The WISDOM
of the
Healing Wound

A New View on Why We Hurt
& How We Can Cure
Even the Deepest Physical
and Emotional Wounds

DAVID KNIGHTON, M.D.

Health Communications, Inc.
Deerfield Beach, Florida

www.hcibooks.com

Library of Congress Cataloging-in-Publication Data

Knighton, David, 1949-
  The wisdom of the healing wound : a new view on why we hurt & how we can cure even the deepest physical and emotional wounds /
David Knighton.
     p. cm.
  Includes bibliographical references and index.
  ISBN-13: 978-0-7573-1561-9 (trade paper)
  ISBN-10: 0-7573-1561-5 (trade paper)
  ISBN-13: 978-0-7573-1597-8 (hardcover)
  ISBN-10: 0-7573-1597-6 (hardcover)
  [etc.]
  1. Mental healing. 2. Mind and body. 3. Self-care, Health. I. Title.
RZ400.K57 2011
615.8'51--dc22

2011007237

Publisher: Health Communications, Inc.
     3201 S.W. 15th Street
     Deerfield Beach, FL 33442–8190

Cover illustration ©Rolffimages/Dreamstime.com
Cover, interior design, and formatting by Lawna Patterson Oldfield

About David Knighton, M.D.

David Knighton is one of the world's leading authorities on wound healing; a visionary medical researcher who has worked with C. Everett Koop, Judah Folkman, Thomas Hunt, and other giants in surgery and medical research; and a highly successful inventor and entrepreneur. His discoveries have generated over a billion dollars in revenue, and he has put most of his own share of this revenue into further research and discovery.

For ten years, David ran the Wound Healing Institute at the University of Minnesota Medical Center, which specialized in healing patients who had been declared unhealable by other doctors. David taught and did research at the University of Minnesota from 1984 to 1992.

In 1984, David founded Curative Technologies, a medical technology company whose products stimulate healing in previously nonhealing wounds. In the years that followed, Curative established 115 wound healing centers around the country.

In 1991, David founded Embro Corporation, a biomedical research and development company that creates new technologies for wound healing, surgery, and treating infectious diseases. Seven years later, David founded Embro Vascular, which developed and commercialized a practical vein harvesting system for heart surgery.

In 1992 and 1993, David was named one of America's top 100 doctors for his work in wound healing. In 1994, he was one of seven experts brought together by the Wound Healing Society to create formal medical definitions of wounding and healing; these definitions continue to be used throughout the world today.

In 2011, David and one of his companies, Creative Water Solutions, received the Governor's Award for Pollution Prevention from the state of Minnesota for the discovery and development of the first green, renewable water treatment process.

David has spoken to hundreds of groups—from social workers to spiritual leaders to college students to physicians—on the topic of healing. He has published hundreds of short pieces in general-interest publications, including the *Chicago Tribune, Science,* the *Chicago Sun-Times,* and *Christianity Today,* as well as 100-plus articles in medical journals such as the *Lancet, Annals of Surgery,* and *Cell and Tissue Research.* He lives in Minneapolis with his wife, Florence.

To the four healers in my life:

My mentor, Tom Hunt, M.D.,
who taught me how the body heals;

Mic Hunter and Gina Lewis,
who helped me heal my psychological wounds;

and, most of all,

My wife, Florence,
who helped heal all of me.

Contents

CHAPTER 1

The Miracle and Mystery of Healing

Wounds are universal. We all experience wounds—to our bodies, our psyches, our spirits, and our relationships. In fact, wounding is such a common experience that we take it for granted as a normal part of life. How many times in a day do you say "ouch"? Each "ouch" is evidence of a wound.

Wounding unites all life. Even molecules can be wounded. The DNA that carries our genetic code is constantly being wounded by cosmic energy and other forces that cut its strands in two, tear off a molecule or two, or destroy whole segments. Luckily for us, our cells have sophisticated emergency systems that recognize the problem and repair the damage.

Without this healing, life would not exist. Yet wounding is every bit as essential to life as healing. In fact, the two work together in an immensely intricate biological dance that permeates all of nature. The processes of evolution and natural selection are all about wounding and healing. The organism that heals most effectively survives to reproduce.

We even wound ourselves for our own benefit. We do this every time we exercise. Our muscles are made up of cells, as well as tiny blood vessels called capillaries. These capillaries carry nutrients to all our cells, and carry away waste products from those cells. When we're at rest, the amount of blood flowing through our capillaries easily provides for every cell's needs. But when we exercise, our muscle cells require many more nutrients to support their increased workload. They also produce more waste that needs to be carried away.

At first our body responds by increasing our heart rate. The arteries that supply blood to our muscles expand, and the microscopic valves that regulate blood flow to our capillaries open wide. But if we keep exercising, we'll feel our muscles burning. This is because each muscle cell's need for nutrients has outstripped our body's ability to supply it with nourishment through the capillary system. Deprived of sufficient oxygen, the muscle cells become wounded. In response, these muscle cells produce signals that tell the body to grow more capillaries in order to provide more nutrients the next time you exercise. The muscle cells also grow a little larger so they can produce more energy.

In short, exercise is a matter of regularly wounding your muscles and letting them heal. Strange as it sounds, wounding yourself helps you stay fit.

Wounds and Memory

Now for an even stranger truth: wounds are a form of memory. They enable your body to store information about where danger lies and when you need to be careful.

Think of the earliest physical cut, scratch, puncture, break, or burn that you can remember. Then mentally relive that incident from beginning to end. Replay the events, the smells, the sights, and the sounds.

Even though this wounding happened many years ago, you probably still have vivid physical and emotional memories of the incident. This is because your mind stored this information in capital letters and flashing neon, so that if a similar situation occurs again, you'll act differently—and, ideally, avoid being wounded again.

A wound may be memorialized in another form as well: a scar. Each scar is a visible—and visceral—reminder from our body, telling us, "Don't do this again!"

On my right index finger is a scar from a deep cut I got from a tin can lid fifty years ago. I was eight years old. I will never forget being cut; bleeding and screaming; my parents washing out the wound; and my father holding me down while my mother poured iodine into the wound. When I think about this almost ancient occurrence, my heart starts to beat faster; I get a visceral ache in the pit of my belly; and anger and fear rise up. Even though this happened over fifty years ago, I can vividly relive the incident.

As we will see, while this process works well when applied to dangerous physical situations, the same ability to recall earlier wounds can create significant psychological scars that affect our relationships years later.

Wounds teach us about who we are, where we have been, and what we need to do in the future. Our wounds thus make us wiser, better able to survive and thrive. Their lessons stick, in part because of the pain of healing, in part because the cost of not learning their lessons can be life threatening.

Wounds are our greatest teachers, our most important survival tools, our best instruments of growth and change, and our most powerful sources of information about life. Paradoxically, wounding is probably our greatest stimulus for health. It is fair to say that wounds are one of God's (or, if you prefer, evolution's) greatest gifts to us.

Getting to Know Wounds

Just what is a wound? The answer is not as simple as you might think.

We all know the obvious wounds: cuts, scrapes, tears, breaks, punctures, burns, and so on. But many wounds are invisible or impalpable, and some have equally invisible or impalpable causes.

In fact, modern science had a terribly hard time coming to agreement about what a wound is. Believe it or not, as late as 1994 there was no clear, universally accepted definition of the word.

That was the year when the newly formed Wound Healing

Society brought together seven experts from a variety of fields to create such a definition. I was one of the seven. The others included two dermatologists, one of whom specialized in wound healing; a plastic surgeon who specialized in burns and burn healing; an internist who specialized in caring for diabetic wounds that wouldn't heal; a nurse who specialized in the care of wounds; and a researcher in wound healing.

Before the meeting began, the plastic surgeon and I guessed that the group would be able to complete the task in a couple of hours. We could not have been more wrong. The process took us through many hours of fractured, grueling, contentious debate. Each medical specialty looked at wounds from its own perspective, with its own definitions, treatments, and biases.

Almost immediately, the intellectual and experiential divide between surgeons and internists became evident. We surgeons held the more limited view. To us, a wound occurred when a physical force impacted tissue and either took some away or split it in two. Wounds were caused by forces we could usually see, understand, and measure. We repaired wounds by either taking out tissue that didn't work or by sewing tissue back together. For us, healing was the process that knitted broken tissue together again.

The internists saw wounds completely differently. They mainly dealt with injury caused by the body attacking itself. This process usually started small, but increased over time until tissue was so damaged that it couldn't function normally.

To the internists, the primary cause of wounds was the process of inflammation. Although inflammation is a critical and natural part of normal wound repair, prolonged and intense inflammation can be as destructive as a bullet wound.

After a very long day, the seven of us agreed on a short, clear, simple definition of wounds that anyone can understand. (The best definitions always turn out that way.) Here is what we came up with:

A wound is the disruption of the normal structure and function of a tissue.

Fifteen years have passed since that conference, and our definition has stood the test of time. It continues to be the definition used by medical professionals throughout the world.

Psychological Wounds

For most of us, psychological wounds occur almost as frequently as physical ones. Most are minor; others are deep; and a few can be life threatening. Some psychological wounds heal quickly and leave no trace, while others produce significant scars that are constant reminders of trauma.

We learn lessons from psychological wounds in the same way we do from physical ones. We learn what behavior not to repeat; what people and situations to avoid; and when and how to protect ourselves.

Is there any difference between physical wounds and psychological ones? Not fundamentally. Like physical wounds, psychological wounds are about the disruption of structure and function. The structure is our interconnectedness with the people, creatures, places, and situations we encounter. The function is our ability to learn, adapt, serve, and grow as we live within that structure.

Think of your many relationships in life. They comprise an ever-widening circle of interactions that start with your birth mother and extend to your family of origin, extended family, friends, pets, classmates, neighbors, coworkers, local community, country, and ultimately the world. This interrelatedness forms an intricate structure similar to the cells, nerves, bones, arteries, and skin of your physical body. The healthy functioning of this social structure is as vital to life as the function of your body. Just like your physical body, this structure can be (and sometimes is) wounded. Those wounds affect your psychological health, as well as the health of the entire social organism.

Psychological wounds do not just affect our emotions, self-worth, and relationships; they can also cause wounds to our physical structure and functioning. As we will see, our psychological state affects many critical pathways necessary to our physical healing. Our physical health often affects the healing of our psychological wounds as well.

The evolution of psychological healing closely parallels that of physical healing. Until the early twentieth century, wounded relationships and emotions were dealt with mainly by shamans, seers, prophets, and clergy. Little was understood about the psyche (just as little was understood about physical wound healing), so psychological healing was left to the realm of the supernatural. What we now call post-traumatic stress disorder was called "soldier's heart" and, later, "shell shock," and little could be done to heal it.

Soon after World War I, however, medicine and psychology made huge parallel advances. Penicillin and other antibiotics were used to support physical healing, and psychologists began to understand many of the complexities of parent-child relationships. By World War II, when the psychological wounds of battle were called "battle fatigue," psychology began to treat this problem as a disease similar to physical wounding.

After the war, the fields of cellular biology and biochemistry evolved dramatically. These enabled the more specialized field of physical wound healing to define and more fully understand the process of normal wound repair. At the same time, our understanding of the causes, effects, and treatment of psychological wounds deepened as well.

In the late 1960s, the discovery of biochemical growth factors, which control the cellular events of wound healing, ushered in a new era in physical wound treatment. Two decades later, the development of eye movement desensitization and reprocessing (EMDR) therapy gave psychologists new tools for treating psychological wounds. EMDR uses rhythmic, alternating sensory inputs from the right side of the body to the left and back again, mimicking rapid eye movement (REM) sleep while the patient is awake. This technique helps the person access images and memories in their subconscious that are blocked from their conscious memory. Using this and other new psychotherapy techniques, old psychological wounds can now be uncovered, cleaned out, and allowed to heal.

Spiritual Wounds

Spiritual wounding and healing are very real phenomena. We each have a spirit that has a relationship with something beyond ourselves. ("Spirit" is not currently an SC—Scientifically Correct—term, however, so feel free to replace it with something you like better.) Call it what you will, the flow of energy between our spirits and the greater source has a structure and a function. It can be nurtured or ignored, wounded or healed.

Nurturing our spiritual connectedness (or whatever we choose to call it) results in serenity, calm, assurance, peace, groundedness, and a sound sense of purpose. My professional and personal experience has shown this to be true, time after time.

Each of us has a space within us that might be called a spiritual receptor system. This system replicates the way our cells communicate with each other.

On the surface of all cells are receptors. These are complex molecules that protrude from each cell's surface. Each receptor has a unique shape so that only a specific molecule will fit into that receptor. It's like a lock and key. When the receptor is triggered by the right molecule, it stimulates the cell to change in a certain way. Some receptors tell the cell to move; others tell it to divide; others tell it to make a specific protein; and so on. Once a receptor is unlocked, it moves inside the cell and is recycled. Our cells are constantly being activated in these ways.

It takes energy for the cell to make receptors, respond to their signals, and recycle them. Healthy cells can produce a great many receptors, and can even increase their number when they are being steadily used up. If a cell is not stimulated, however, it typically goes into a resting or dormant state; if this lack of stimulation continues, the cell eventually dies. So receptors not only tell the cell what to do but keep it stimulated and healthy.

Now imagine a parallel spiritual receptor system. When we allow our spiritual receptors to be unlocked—through nature, music, art, giving of ourselves, prayer, meditation, and so on—we experience deep joy, peace, and serenity. When we shut off the flow of spiritual connectedness, however, we first can go into a dormant spiritual state; then, if the spiritual drought lasts too long, our spirit will atrophy and possibly die.

Today, even many agnostic and atheist doctors recognize the validity of spiritual healing. Some, who object to the word "spiritual," say something like, "The force behind this healing is not yet understood." Fair enough. But whatever it is and whatever people choose to call it, they acknowledge its reality.

The Twelve Step programs of addiction recovery provide excellent examples of spiritual healing. Addiction has long been an intractable problem that both medicine and psychology attempted to address, with very limited success. Only about 10–20 percent of addicts who receive non-Twelve Step treatments recover from their addictions. In contrast, Twelve Step programs have a much higher success rate, about 30–50 percent.

Twelve Step programs recognize the importance of including a Higher Power in the healing process. Interestingly, it doesn't matter what this Higher Power is called, how it's defined, whether it's synonymous with God, or even whether the addict understands it. What's important is simply acknowledging a power beyond ourselves that can help us to change and to heal our spiritual and psychological wounds.

All three types of wounding and healing are interconnected. Physical wounding affects our psychological and spiritual health; psychological wounding has physical and spiritual ramifications; and spiritual wounding can impact our psychological and physical health.

Wounds and Pain

In physical wounding, pain is almost always the first signal that something is not right.

Embedded in our skin are specialized nerves that sense pain. Certain areas of the body, such as our fingertips, face, and genitalia, have many pain-sensing nerves, and are therefore exquisitely sensitive to pain.

At least, this is the case in healthy people. People with some serious illnesses can lose this essential survival tool. I once had a patient who suffered from severe diabetes, with all its complications. He was blind, had kidney failure that required a transplant, had artery disease that kept some wounds from healing, and had severe neuropathy that made his feet totally numb.

One day when he came to see me, he was surrounded by an overpowering stench. The soles of his feet were black and the area between the dead, dried skin and the rest of his foot oozed pus. "What happened?" I asked. He explained that he'd been in California, racing his dragster. It was 100 degrees and he stood on the black asphalt in his tennis shoes. The hot asphalt heated the bottom of his shoes, and then the soles of his feet, to the point that he completely burned his skin. Yet he felt nothing; the destruction of his nerves by diabetes had made his feet totally numb.

Most of our critical internal structures are also loaded with pain-sensing nerves. Arteries and veins cause intense pain when they are stretched or damaged. The tissue covering our bones contains pain fibers that warn of the impending disruption of our skeletal foundation. Without this early-warning system of pain, we would not know when we are being wounded, and we would thus be more likely to die of those wounds.

Psychological wounds also cause pain. When someone makes a nasty or sarcastic remark to us, we might respond, "Hey, that hurts!" This isn't mere metaphor; the pain is real. Psychological and physical wounds stimulate some of the very same areas of the brain.

Just as physical pain makes us recoil from the cause of a wound, psychological pain also makes us recoil from its cause. Furthermore, just as repeated stresses on our physical skin cause us to form calluses, we may respond to repeated psychological stresses by developing psychological calluses that create a protective barrier. Severe and repeated psychological trauma can also lead to emotional numbness—or, in the most serious cases, to the blunting of our ability to heal.

Spiritual wounding causes a third type of pain: the pain of disconnection and atrophy. When our flow of spiritual energy is chronically diminished, we feel spiritual pain—typically experienced as emptiness, a void, or a deep hunger. Reopening the flow of spiritual energy replenishes the spiritual receptors, stops the pain, and restores health.

One way to picture this flow of spiritual energy is to imagine your arteries. Arteries carry oxygenated, nutrition-filled blood to all our tissues. But artery walls can be wounded, scarred, and stretched, just like skin. When an artery narrows because of scarring, restricting the flow of blood, we call this wounding atherosclerosis. As the flow diminishes, the surrounding tissue becomes starved. This creates significant pain, signaling that something is terribly wrong.

As a vascular surgeon, I have cared for many patients with poor arterial flow. If it comes on gradually, the pain slowly increases. If it occurs all at once, the pain is intense. Patients tell me it is far worse than any other pain they have ever experienced. And no wonder: their tissues are dying.

In similar fashion, scarring in our spiritual arteries can gradually restrict the energy flow to our spiritual receptors, causing gradually increasing pain if the process is slow, and excruciating pain if the flow is cut off abruptly.

Wounds and Scarring

You can easily write a short history of your life just by looking at all your scars, and reviewing them in the order in which you received them.

Not every wound leaves a scar, however. Minor wounds that don't penetrate the fat under the skin usually don't scar. New skin cells grow over the divot, and after a few weeks the wounded area is back to normal.

In humans and other mammals, deeper wounds always produce scars. These begin as hard tissue that glues the two sides of a wound together. At first most scars are pronounced, raised, and often tender. As time passes and a scar matures, however, it slowly flattens, blends in with the surrounding tissue, and becomes progressively less tender.

A wound in an area that frequently moves—a joint, for example—can become repeatedly re-wounded with each motion. This often creates a wide, prominent scar. The most extreme case of this is an inflammatory disease called myositis ossificans. This devastating disease wounds muscles; because they move so frequently, they are almost constantly re-wounded. As each muscle heals, the body deposits calcium in it, slowly turning it to stone. This scarring is ultimately fatal.

Like their physical counterparts, small psychological wounds usually heal quickly, leave no scars, and are soon forgotten. However, deeper psychological wounds must heal in stages, just like physical wounds, and the end result is psychological scarring. If the healing is quick and thorough, the psychological scar becomes supple and almost insignificant. But if the same area is wounded over and over, a large and painful scar—typically some form of neurosis or dysfunction—often results.

Many mental and physical diseases can disrupt, delay, or harden psychological scars to the point where normal, productive daily life becomes impossible. Severe and repeated psychological trauma can even turn people into emotional stone, like myositis ossificans.

Yet even very serious wounds—whether physical, psychological, or spiritual—can be repaired.

Luckily, we do not have to stand by and helplessly watch an illness progress. Consider the case of another of my patients with diabetes. The illness had seriously limited the blood flow to his left foot. He'd lost a couple of toes, but I partially restored the flow through bypass surgery, attaching a vein and making it into an artery. Over the years, however, his foot gradually worsened as the illness steadily closed off the bypass until it stopped functioning entirely. However, since I knew that massage gradually increased blood flow through small, newly formed arteries, I asked this patient and his wife to massage his foot and leg, while picturing them getting warmer and warmer. They both rigorously followed this routine, and she also added daily prayer. Gradually his blood flow improved, the foot warmed, and the pain decreased to the point where he went off pain medication and the bypass started to function again. (I confirmed this with arterial tests.) I don't know whether it was the massage, the visualization, the prayer, or all three that created this deep healing. But this patient lived the rest of his life with a painless foot.

Like our physical body, our spirit is covered by a sort of skin that surrounds and protects the flow of energy. Like physical muscles, this skin becomes healthier and thicker with use and training. As it strengthens, it also becomes more resistant to wounding—and, if it does become wounded, it heals more rapidly with proper care. However, neglected spiritual skin becomes thin and easily damaged.

Frequent wounding of our spiritual skin, just like our psychological and physical skin, results in scarring. It loses its structure and function. The flow of spiritual energy can slow to a trickle, resulting in spiritual starvation. Whether this flow can ever be completely cut off is debatable. It may be that our spiritual arteries can be severely restricted but never completely closed off. However, with the proper care and stimulus, even those spiritual arteries that have been seriously restricted for long periods of time can be brought back to life. Our scarred spiritual arteries can reopen just like my patient's vein bypass—perhaps not in every single case, but often. Just how they open and what causes them to do so are still largely unknown. But such reopening is real, measurable, and documentable. Later chapters of this book will look at this subject in more detail.

Scarring is normal, but it is not universal. You probably know that newts, starfish, and certain other lower animals can regenerate severed limbs without producing scars. But human fetuses can also heal from wounds without scarring. This enables pediatric surgeons to fix congenital defects while a baby is still in the uterus. (Interestingly, as soon as a baby is born, the healing response changes so that wounding creates scarring.) Someday soon we hope to understand this process well enough to induce similar healing in children and adults.

What Is Healing?

When the Wound Healing Society brought us seven professionals together, its leaders also asked us to define healing. This was much easier. If a wound is *a disruption of normal structure and function*, then we knew that healing is *the restoration of structure and function*.

Notice that the word "normal" does not appear in our definition of healing. That wasn't an oversight. Although healing usually restores the wounded area to *almost* a normal, healthy state, in mature mammals it never regains *totally* normal structure and function.

The quality of healing can vary widely from person to person, and even from wound to wound. It depends on many variables, such as the location of the wound on the body, the extent and depth of the wound, whether the wound has smooth or ragged edges, whether it is clean or contaminated, the health and age of the person, the medications they are taking, and so on. Physicians and surgeons are constantly humbled by wounds in some patients that heal poorly, slowly, or not at all. After thousands of years of medical advancement, we still tell each other the same thing healers have said for many dozens of generations: "Only God can heal it." A surgeon makes a wound, closes it, does what they can to nurture its healing, and must leave the rest to powers beyond our control.

Until about 300 years ago, the three areas of healing—physical, psychological, and spiritual—were seen as one and the same. As modern science evolved, however, it eventually separated the three into distinct areas of study. Biology and medicine focused on the physical aspects of healing, psychology on the emotional aspects, and theology on the spiritual. As each field of study advanced, its understanding of the complexity of the human body, mind, and spirit resulted in further compartmentalization of cause and effect. Medicine shifted from a healing profession to a mechanistic synthesis of diagnosis and therapy. Psychology gradually mapped human relationships and the subconscious mind, and related them to psychological health (and psychological disorders). Theology focused on understanding and cataloging our relationship with God. Eventually the pendulum swung all the way to the scientific side, with medical science dismissing spiritual and psychological forms of healing as quackery.

Now, thankfully, the pendulum is once again swinging back toward a more balanced view—one that embraces the physical, the psychological, *and* the spiritual, and that acknowledges the unity of all three. Indeed, the three different types of wounds all serve the same purpose: to teach us, to help us survive, and to enable us to grow, heal, and stay healthy.

Knowledge vs. Wisdom

We now know far more about wounds and healing than we did even ten years ago. In another decade our knowledge will likely double yet again.

But knowledge alone is not enough. To heal, we also need the wisdom to apply our knowledge in the right way.

The dilemma of a patient I treated some years ago can serve as an example. I was working at the University of Minnesota Wound Healing Institute, seeing patients whose wounds would not heal. The patient was a very healthy-looking young woman with no visible wounds. Yet her life was falling apart. Her marriage was in trouble and she wondered if she was going crazy.

Her problems began soon after the birth of her first child, who was now over a year old. Her pregnancy went smoothly, but she had a long and exhausting labor that required a lot of pushing. Her baby was born healthy, but because the labor was so difficult, her OB-GYN performed an episiotomy just before the birth. This involves cutting the vaginal wall and the surrounding skin with scissors to make the opening bigger and keep the skin from tearing. It's a relatively common procedure. After the birth, the doctor sewed up the cut in the usual manner, and the woman left the hospital without a problem.

About six weeks later, her vagina became very tender and extremely sensitive to even the slightest pressure. Simply sitting in the wrong position caused her great pain. Sex was excruciating, and quickly became out of the question.

For the first few weeks after the birth, her OB-GYN told her not to worry, that the pain was not unusual and would soon go away. Three months later, however, the pain was stronger than ever. She couldn't bear to have the area around the incision touched. She consulted her OB-GYN, who again told her that nothing was wrong and she shouldn't worry.

When the problem persisted, she visited a variety of M.D.s. All her vaginal exams proved normal. Unable to find any physical problem, the doctors told her that emotional stress was likely the problem.

As the woman told me this part of her story, she began to cry.

"I'm in constant pain," she said. "I can't make love to my husband, and they're telling me it's all in my head!"

As she spoke, I pictured the healing of her incision. Doctors usually use an absorbable suture—that is, one that slowly dissolves into the body—to close the wound. I knew that some sutures dissolve better than others, and I guessed her problem had something to do with an undissolved suture.

I told her I would need to carefully examine the wounded area. She agreed, and a clinic nurse helped her into a gown and onto the exam table.

All the tissues around her vagina looked normal, and the episiotomy scar was well healed. But when I gently touched the area, she almost came off the table. Slowly, I helped her relax and let the tissues get used to my examining fingers. Once the tight muscles in the area had relaxed, I found a small, hard spot that was extraordinarily tender. I knew then that she had an undissolved suture knot that was probably surrounded with inflammatory cells, desperately trying to remove the knot from her body.

One week later she came in for surgery, and I found exactly what I thought I would find. I made a small incision in the tissue over the knot, and immediately a small drop of pus came out, followed by a suture knot.

This woman's body had been in a year-long standoff with the suture. It would not dissolve because the enzymes that normally cause this material to dissolve were not strong enough to complete the job. The knot then became a foreign substance that her body tried to kill. When it couldn't make the suture go away, her body walled it off. The trapped inflammatory cells kept trying to get rid of the knot, and, in the process, produced substances that caused pain.

At her one-week follow-up visit, my patient was a changed woman. Her husband was with her, and they couldn't wait to tell me that the pain was gone and she had already had vaginal sex with very little pain. Her husband thanked me for saving their marriage, and she thanked me for not thinking she was crazy.

How This Book Can Help

This book is for anyone who has been wounded—in other words, everyone.

All of us have been wounded physically, psychologically, and spiritually. We have healed from most of these wounds, but we all bear their scars. Most of us also carry with us wounds of all three types that have not yet healed.

This book is about deepening—and perhaps completing—your healing. It will help you to:

- Understand how your wounds serve, support, and teach you.
- Learn how the human organism heals—and sometimes fails to heal.
- Best support your own physical, psychological, and spiritual healing.
- Better understand the often-mysterious process of spiritual healing.
- Learn about little-known but profoundly effective

treatments for healing physical, psychological, and spiritual wounds.

- See wounds, healing, and health in a new and life-affirming way.

I'm not a magician or a miracle worker, however—just an experienced surgeon. Not that I haven't witnessed miracles. In fact, I've seen quite a few, and I've been part of many others. But not one of those miracles was my own doing. Sometimes I asked for help, opened myself up to the unknown, and watched a miracle unfold. At other times, miracles happened in spite of my foolish and egotistical efforts to control the situation. You'll read about a few of these miracles in this book.

You'll also read some true stories of healing that resulted not from miracles, but from careful research, creative thinking, and smart medical sleuthing.

This book also contains some true stories of mistakes I and other medical professionals made. You can learn much about healing from these stories as well.

Ultimately, this book is about being human—about living fully as body, mind, and spirit. More important, it is about the powerful, transformative, and often surprising ways we can heal and thrive in the face of our wounds.

I invite you to join me on this deeply healing, deeply human journey.

CHAPTER 2

How Cells
Live, Talk, and Work

The trillions of cells that make up a human body all work, communicate, and move about, just as human beings do. All of these activities are vital to the process of healing.

If you were to shrink down to the size of a molecule and stand inside a cell, you'd see that it is a walled city with many thousands of residents. Each resident is a molecule, with its own clear structure and function. If you were to stand outside that cell, however, you'd see that it is one small member of an enormous galaxy of cells.

Let's take a closer look at what goes on inside this walled microcity.

Each cell in your body has its particular function. Some cells produce products that are used by other cells. Some protect the human body from foreign invasion and death. Some detect what belongs inside the body and what is foreign. Some process information at lightning speed; others store that information. Some provide motion. Some create pipelines that transport life-giving blood or remove wastes. Some cells pump. Some filter. Some pass on the genetic code that allows you to have children. And some orchestrate this whole grand production.

Like you and me, cells eat, digest, and produce waste. A cell eats by surrounding its food (certain desirable molecules) with a portion of its wall, just as you'd put your mouth around a grape. The cell then brings the molecules inside in a pinching motion, not unlike chomping down on that grape. Once the molecules are inside, the cell opens them up and their contents are absorbed, just as the juice and pulp of the grape would slide down your throat and get digested. The scientific name for this process is endocytosis.

Now imagine the same process in reverse. This is how cells get rid of waste materials. They spit out what they don't want, and the waste products are carried away by the bloodstream to organs that dispose of them.

Cells also (metaphorically) drink and urinate. They do this through a slow, passive process called diffusion. In diffusion, molecules move from an area of high concentration to one of low concentration.

Imagine that you squeeze a drop of ink onto the center of a

paper towel. As you watch, the ink makes a stain in the middle, then slowly travels outward in an ever-lightening circle.

Now picture a pen that continuously drips ink on the same spot. The circle widens steadily as more and more ink is deposited in the center. However, it remains darkest at the center and gradually lightens as you move further toward the edge. This is diffusion in action.

Almost every cell contains a nucleus that serves as its administrative center. Inside each nucleus is a library of blueprints for that cell. These blueprints are called DNA, and they never leave the nucleus. But the cell is able to make copies, which can be passed on to other cells.

The Work Life and Sex Life of a Cell

Many of the cells in your body are constantly in motion. Some are carried throughout the body, suspended in blood. Others move by crawling on a molecular surface like a snail. Other cells move by contraction, just like muscles. Some cells sway back and forth to sense sound waves and the movement of our bodies.

Communication is critical for cells, just as it is for people and cultures. Cells communicate by touching each other and sending each other chemical messages, called cytokines. Each type of cytokine (and there are thousands of types) is unique, and most cells have thousands of different kinds of receptors for recognizing cytokines. Each receptor is attuned to one particular cytokine (though sometimes multiple types of receptors in the same cell are attuned to the same cytokine, just as you can tune a roomful of radios to the same station). Once a cytokine encounters the right kind of receptor, it triggers chemical changes in the cell that tell the cell what to do. There are cytokines that tell cells to divide, move, become a different kind of cell, or produce a new molecule.

The process of wound healing depends on all these messages being sent and delivered properly. When cellular communication fails or gets scrambled, cells die or divide out of control; tissues don't do their jobs correctly; and organs fall out of sync with the rest of the body. These snafus can cause illness or death.

Cells in different tissues behave differently depending on whether they stand alone or touch neighboring cells. In fact, some cells are programmed to move around until they touch an identical cell. When that happens, they settle down, attach to each other, quit dividing, and start performing their designated function together.

In most parts of your body—especially your skin and your digestive system—cells are continuously wearing out, dying, and being replaced by fresh cells. In fact, most cells have a defined life span. Like human beings, and all plants and animals visible to the naked eye, they are genetically programmed to grow old and die.

We humans usually survive for only three or four generations. We live to kiss our grandchildren, and often our great-grand-children, but rarely our great-great-grandchildren. Most normal cells in your body, however, can live for up to fifty generations.

One dangerous exception is cancer. Cancer cells can live and divide indefinitely, which is why they pose such a potential threat to the human body.

Like people, cells can also die young—through infection, trauma, autoimmune destruction, or environmental damage. When a cell dies, the body normally creates a replacement. Recently, scientists have discovered that most tissues in the body contain resident stem cells that slowly replace injured or dead cells.

Cells reproduce by dividing into two, in a magnificent symphony. First, the cell makes a copy of its DNA, which is a double strand of genes containing the cell's genetic code. Then these two DNA partners do a dance in which they line up opposite each other. A strand of protein attaches to each gene inside each set of DNA. This protein strand pulls everything apart, creating two identical nuclei inside the cell wall. The climax of the symphony comes when the cell wall splits the cell in half, creating two identical daughter cells.

All human cells reproduce in this way, with two exceptions: sperm cells and egg cells. These divide in a unique way that allows each cell to contribute exactly 50 percent (rather than the usual 100 percent) of the DNA of a normal cell. Instead of making two completely new sets of DNA, they each give half the necessary DNA to each new cell. This is how a sperm and an egg create an embryonic stem cell (and, if all goes well, an embryo and then a baby) that carries genetic material from each parent. It's called a stem cell because all other cells in the human body grow from it, just as the many branches of a tree grow from its trunk.

Stem Cells

Each of us starts out as a stem cell, which contains genetic material from both our parents. The sperm from our father contributes a random sample of half his DNA, and the egg in our mother contributes a random sample of half her DNA. These unite to form a single stem cell (sometimes called a zygote), which quickly divides into two stem cells. These divide into four, then eight, and so on, until they number in the tens of millions.

To become a human being with trillions of cells, this original stem cell reproduces itself trillions of times. At first, it divides into more stem cells. Over the generations, however, these cells morph into all the different cell types needed by the body.

What tells embryonic stem cells to divide, and how do they know when and where to change from a stem cell into something different? Science isn't sure yet, but current experiments have begun to yield some answers. We do know that two very different factors are involved: the molecules that tell the cells to grow, move, and divide, called *growth factors*, and the local cellular environment. You'll recognize this as the nature vs. nurture, or genetics vs. environment, argument played out on a cellular level. (As we'll see in the next chapter, these molecules are not only essential to human growth and development, they're equally necessary for health and healing.)

At certain points in a fetus's development, other kinds of cells begin to form, branching off from the stem cells. Scientists call this process differentiation. Each different type of cell follows a unique pathway toward its ultimate function. For example, some cells become bone cells; others, bone marrow cells; others, blood cells; others, brain cells; and so on and on. Once a certain type of cell—a muscle cell, let's say—branches off from a cluster of stem cells, it divides into two muscle cells, then four muscle cells, then eight. These cells continually divide to repopulate the body with their own offspring. Some of these cells branch out further, changing into a more specific type of cell. For example, some stem cells become the iris of your eye, some become the cornea, and some become the retina.

In some parts of the human body, stem cells stay dormant until replacement cells are needed. For example, the liver stays relatively stable until part of it is removed or damaged, at which point its stem cells start to divide in order to replace the missing piece. When the liver has regrown to its original size, the cells stop dividing and become dormant once more. This is equally true for a human fetus, a growing child, and a grown adult.

Until a few years ago, it was widely believed that some parts of the human body, particularly the brain and heart, stopped producing stem cells after birth, and other parts stopped producing them once someone reached adulthood. Medical science believed that these organs gradually aged and wore out, until finally the person died. Recent research, however, has proven that stem cells live almost everywhere in a normal adult or child's body—including their brain and heart—ready to grow fresh, new tissue. (There are some exceptions, such as hair, nails, teeth, etc.) Under the right circumstances, these stem cells divide and repopulate the organ with new, healthy cells.

These are not the same as embryonic stem cells, which can turn into any part of the body. Instead, they are what we call *adult peripheral stem cells* (or, more simply, *adult stem cells*), which can only repopulate specific organs and tissues.

A third type of stem cell, called *wound-derived stem cells*, has very recently been discovered. This stem cell also comes from adults and children—but it appears to be able to become almost any type of cell in the body, just like embryonic stem cells. I'll discuss this type of stem cell in detail, and say more about stem cells in general, in Chapter 8.

As I write this chapter, a debate rages over the ethics of using human embryonic stem cells in medical research. Very soon— perhaps by the time you read this book—the debate will have ended, because we will routinely harvest and use stem cells from adults and children, making the use of embryonic stem cells unnecessary.

Over the past decade, stem cell research has vastly increased, and in the years to come it will expand ever faster, particularly once we make the transition to using only adult and/or wound-derived stem cells. Stem cells have already been used to grow new tissues in the laboratory, and to help people heal more quickly.

In a very few years, stem cell therapy will dramatically increase the speed at which broken bones, cuts, and other external wounds can heal. But that is only the beginning. Current research suggests that stem cells can be used to treat many diseases, such as diabetes, Parkinson's disease, heart disease, retinal diseases, and healing disorders.

My own research lab has been working with stem cells since 2005. We have used adult rat stem cells to help rats heal from lab-induced wounds far more quickly than normal. We will soon begin to test this technique on men and women. If we get similar results in people, then in a very few years we may live in a world where healing from illness and injury typically takes half as long as it does today.

CHAPTER 3

How Your Body Heals

Have you ever cut yourself and wondered how your whole body knows it's been injured? Have you ever marveled at how orderly the process of healing is?

If you pay attention the next time you get a minor cut, you will observe the miracle of wound healing. Notice how the pain is immediate and how your body involuntarily recoils to limit the damage. Notice how you instantly have a sick feeling in the pit of your belly. If the cut is on your hand or finger, notice how you instinctively put it to your mouth and suck on the wound—and how the pain around the cut reminds you to protect the area from further damage.

The next day, notice that the area is swollen and a little pink. A moist, clear fluid oozes from the center of the cut. Notice how any movement of the tissue around the cut causes pain, reminding you to leave it alone and keep it still.

As the day proceeds, notice how the pain slowly subsides. You still know something is not right, but the wound doesn't scream when touched.

The third day after the cut, notice that it is covered with a hard shell. If you try to peel this shell away, the pain tells you to stop. When you gently feel around the cut, it is slightly raised and hard.

On the fourth day, the pain is almost gone. The hard scab is loosening at the edges. You can use that area of skin without any problem or pain.

During the next few days, the skin cells start to grow under the scab. Soon the scab comes off, and the new skin is pink and tender to the touch.

In the days after that, a thick layer of tough callused skin grows over the new tender skin to protect it. Then, after it's grown in, that callus slowly peels away, leaving normal skin (if the cut didn't go into the fat underneath) or a scar (if it did).

Keep watching over the next two weeks and you will see the wounded tissue slowly change. Eventually it loses all pain, but feels a little numb when touched. Notice how you instinctively massage the area and how the desire to press on it eventually disappears.

In doing all this, you are connecting to a cycle of life similar to your breath and heartbeat. It's a slower process, but it's just as critical to sustaining life.

In this chapter we'll look in detail at some of the cellular and biochemical magic you have just witnessed. Although everything that follows is based on sound science, you'll see that it's not at all a mechanical process, but profound and awe-inspiring. While it can get complicated at times, you don't need to try to learn it all. My purpose is to help you better appreciate the biological genius and intricate dance of the healing response. Nothing that follows requires any scientific background or training, and I've used plenty of metaphors to help the magic shine through more clearly.

That said, if you do find yourself getting lost or distracted, feel free to skip ahead to the next paragraph or section. So long as you get a taste of the wonder and beauty behind our ability to heal, you will have experienced the essentials of this chapter.

The Wound Space

A wound always creates an open space. Remember the definition of a wound? *A wound is a disruption in the normal structure and function of a tissue.*

From the vantage point of a cell, what looks to us like an insignificant scrape is devastation. Imagine that you are a skin cell. You spend much of your time making keratin, a major component of calluses, nails, and animal hooves. Occasionally you divide to replace the cells around you that have left.

Suddenly, an enormous, sharp, hard object falls from the area above and penetrates down to your level. Then, as fast as it came, it leaves. Many of your fellow cells are suddenly gone. Worse, the barrier that defined inside from outside, that protected the

How Your Body Heals   35

machinery of life from destruction, has now been breached. It's as if the wall around an ancient city has been broken through. This break in the barrier creates an open space—and an emergency.

Now let's imagine that this cut gets sewn up. One common misconception about healing is that once a wound is stitched up, there is no more wound space. Actually, the wound space is not only still there, but eventually becomes larger than the initial area of tissue destruction.

Let's look at it from the cell's perspective again. First, the cells at the edge of the wound space are damaged from the wounding. In addition, because the blood vessels at the edge of the wound have been severed, all the cells that were fed from those blood vessels die from a lack of oxygen and essential nutrients. From the cell's perspective, a sutured wound is like two people standing on opposite edges of the Grand Canyon trying to communicate with each other. It's an enormous gap.

For centuries scientists have known that nature abhors a void or a vacuum. Whenever possible, once a space is created, it is quickly filled with something. In the body, sometimes a wound space is filled with beneficial, healing components; but it can also fill with bacteria, toxins, or foreign material. These can be difficult, and sometimes impossible, to remove.

Getting bruised also creates a wound space. When you drop a heavy object on your foot, or run into a low table, or tear your muscle playing football, a microscopic wound space is created.

To understand bruising, it is helpful to envision that you are a specialized cell in the fatty tissue under your skin. You've rolled up and formed a microscopic tube. Two of your neighbor cells join with you, together making a micro-pipe that carries blood. (This micro-pipe is called a capillary.)

Suddenly, your world is disrupted by a massive blow. The sudden movement splits you in two, and blood flows into the tissue around you.

Since the pressure pushing the blood through capillaries is low, the bleeding stops quickly, leaving a small space filled with blood cells and a fluid called plasma. The skin roof over your head is intact, but a wound has occurred in your area and must be healed. There is a very visible wound space before you, just as with a cut.

The Battle for Supremacy

When a physical wound that breaks the skin layer occurs, the wound space is immediately exposed to millions upon millions of bacteria. The body's response will determine whether the invaders are held at bay and a protective wall of skin and keratin is rebuilt, or the invaders overwhelm the area, destroy it, and plunder its riches. This epic battle for supremacy takes place within the wound space.

Think of the battle scenes from *The Lord of the Rings* or *Star Wars*, with warriors on both sides stretching across a vast landscape from horizon to horizon. From the viewpoint of one of your body's cells, that's exactly what the battle of healing looks like. On one side are your early responder cells, an elite defensive force with the capacity to eat and destroy untold millions of invading bacteria. On the other side are quickly expanding masses of bacteria that invade the wound space and feed off the debris of the destroyed tissue, such as spent blood cells.

In this battle, there is no good, no evil, no hero, and no villain —only organisms responding in the ancient dance of life and death.

Most of the time, bacteria are enormously helpful to us. When we're healthy, bacteria participate in a finely tuned, perfectly balanced interplay that benefits both them and us. In fact, bacteria cover almost every exposed surface of our bodies, thriving in microscopic colonies. Bacteria cover our skin; the mucous membranes in our mouth, nose, and throat; the airways into our lungs; and our entire digestive tract. These bacterial communities are vital to the healthy functioning of many of our systems. Perhaps the most important thing they do is help us to digest food, breaking it down into molecules we can use.

Bacteria are also nature's recycling system. When an organism of any kind dies, the resident bacteria immediately begin dismantling it into its component parts, returning them back to the earth and air, to be used again in the circle of life.

However, when a wound is created, bacteria become our enemies rather than our allies. Because they cannot tell one dead organism from another, they rush into the wound and do their best to dismantle everything in and around it. Unless our body can defend the wound space, it will rapidly fill up with ravenous bacteria. It will become infected.

As this battle rages in the wound space, the health of the area hangs in the balance. The ultimate outcome will be either healing, and the return of normal structure and function, or infection and tissue death.

Think of a seesaw on a playground. Imagine that the bacteria and foreign bodies are on one side and your body's defenses are on the other. If your defenses outperform the bacteria, they tip your body's balance toward healing. However, if the bacterial invasion outperforms your body's defenses, the seesaw tips in the other direction, toward tissue death.

Sometimes neither side gains an advantage and the two sides stay perfectly balanced. Then no one wins; the bacteria aren't killed, but the wound is not healed, either. Normal structure and function do not return and the local area of infection is contained. This stalemate can last a long time—often with serious consequences.

As we will see in later chapters, many of the therapies we use to treat wounds focus on tipping this balance in favor of healing, by decreasing either the amount of damaged tissue or the number of bacteria. In contrast, many diseases that impair healing, such as HIV/AIDS and diabetes, blunt the body's defenses, tipping the balance in favor of bacteria.

The Body's Defenses

Let's imagine you cut your finger with a knife. It's nothing serious, but you start to bleed, and your finger hurts. At the moment you wound yourself, two systems are activated. First, broken nerves activate your reflexes, causing your muscles to involuntarily flex.

Without thinking—in fact, without even realizing you're doing it—you pull your hand away, limiting the amount of damage. A split second later, pain centers in your brain are activated, making you shout, "Ouch!" or "Damn!"—also without thinking. This may feel like just an expression of surprise and displeasure, but there's a survival purpose behind it: it alerts people around you that you've been hurt and may need assistance.

Your pain centers also trigger what's called a neuro-endocrine feedback loop—or, more commonly, a fight, flight, or freeze response. This marshals all your body's resources to deal with the emergency. Your heart pumps faster; your energy stores are accessed; and all your senses are heightened.

Meanwhile, in the blood vessels in and around the wound, a whole cascade of events has begun, all focused on stopping the bleeding.

Circulating in your blood are trillions of microscopic droids, called platelets. Each droid is pre-programmed to respond to chemical signals in the surrounding area. Most of the time, these droids simply float along. But if they sense that the lining of nearby blood vessels has been disrupted, they spring into action, releasing their healing biochemicals. Some of these molecular messages tell the surrounding blood vessels to contract and shut off blood flow; others tell the platelets to stick together to form a clot; and others, as we'll see later, start the cascade of tissue repair.

This disruption of the blood vessels also activates a second set of molecules that cause clotting. These molecules are in the clear portion of blood called plasma. Within a normal blood vessel, they are held in check by a complex cascade of inhibitors that prevent them from assembling into a clot. When they are exposed to the tissue outside the blood vessel, however, they spin a dense web of material called fibrin that combines with the platelets to fill the wound. The combination of platelets and fibrin helps stop the bleeding.

Your larger blood vessels are also called into battle. These have muscle cells that enable their walls to respond to injury by contracting. This helps close off damaged blood vessels to limit the amount of blood lost. (In a similar, simultaneous response, you may instinctively put pressure on the cut by holding it tight and elevating it, thus limiting your blood loss.)

While all this is going on, another set of specialized proteins, called the complement cascade, also goes to work. It enters the wound, triggering specialized proteins that form a coating around anything foreign—bacteria, dirt, rust, fungus, hair, and so on. This coating, called opsin, is like a uniform. It helps soldiers in battle tell one side from the other. If a particle is covered with opsin, it's considered an intruder.

The Healing Power of Inflammation

Two types of cells respond very quickly to wounding: neutrophils and macrophages. Both types start out as stem cells in your bone marrow. When they are exposed to the right protein molecule, they mature and enter the bloodstream, where they circulate until they are needed. They roam through miles and miles of blood vessels and lymph channels, until they are dumped into a wound by a severed blood vessel, or are drawn into the wound by biochemical messages produced by either the clotting system or the platelet droids.

The neutrophils are the cellular Marines, arriving at the wound space first, storming ashore, and securing the area. Like tough, fearless, battle-hardened soldiers, they have one mission: to remove dead cells, foreign material, and, especially, bacteria.

The neutrophils quickly enter the wound space and look for anything that your plasma has coated with opsin. They recognize all the coated particles, engulf the invaders, and release enzymes to dissolve them.

Neutrophils can gather and increase their numbers very quickly. In a few minutes, their number can grow from thousands to millions. They are also amazingly efficient and tenacious. Most remarkably, they know exactly what is foreign and therefore must be destroyed, and what is part of your body and must be left alone.

Macrophages follow the neutrophils into the wound space after about twenty-four hours. Macrophages are the body's army. After the Marines have started driving the enemy out of the wound, the army takes over, defending and rebuilding the area. This includes cleaning up the debris left over from the earlier battle; finishing the job of subduing the enemy; supplying nutrition and oxygen; removing waste; and installing new lines of communication. Macrophages also act as the central command in the healing process, constantly surveying the environment for invaders and coordinating the rebuilding effort.

In addition to the macrophages circulating in the blood, there are also resident macrophages. These are soldiers living in outposts in specific body tissues, such as a lung or a kidney or the brain. They are ready to spring into action the moment foreign invaders, like bacteria, come into close contact.

Just like neutrophils, macrophages recognize foreign invaders, engulf them, and secrete powerful molecules that destroy them. When in this killing mode, they also send out signals that recruit more macrophages from the bloodstream, and tell the nearby blood vessels to expand to maximum capacity, so that reinforcements, nutrients, and oxygen can be efficiently delivered to the battle site and debris can be carried away. (These signals are what cause inflammation—making the tissue around a newly formed wound look pink or red. Next time you see this halo of pink tissue, root for the macrophages that are calling for reinforcements.)

Interestingly, although macrophages can both attack and repair, they cannot do both at the same time. At any one moment, each macrophage is in either fighting mode or rebuilding mode. As long as there are bacteria to be killed, or dead tissue to remove, the macrophages will signal the body to remain on high alert. Then, once the cleanup is complete, they switch off the high-alert signal and start the rebuilding phase of wound repair.

Rebuilding the Wounded Tissue

This second act in the drama of wound healing is called the proliferative phase. This phase of the battle is about reconstructing the destroyed tissue and returning it to near-normal structure and function as quickly as possible.

The moment your body is wounded, it sends messenger molecules everywhere. These biochemically shout, "Emergency! We need a repair crew NOW!"

The technical name for these messenger molecules is *cytokines*. These are complex, folded proteins that can activate all kinds of responses in cells throughout your body. The messenger molecules that activate specific aspects of the healing response are called *growth factors*, because they were first discovered when scientists sought to answer the question, "What makes cells move and divide?"

There are thousands of different types of growth factors. Each delivers a different message, because each interacts with cells in a unique way. Furthermore, some interact only with certain types of cells. Each growth factor also causes something unique to happen in the body. Many of these thousands of different molecules are needed to successfully rebuild the tissue in any wound space.

Growth factors act locally in the tissue at a wound's edge. They are produced or secreted in the wound space and then diffuse through the fluid-filled spaces around cells. As they diffuse further and further away from their source, they steadily decrease in concentration, forming what is called a chemical gradient.

Remember the process of diffusion from Chapter 2, in which you imagined a pen dripping ink, drop by drop, on a paper towel? The ink makes a circular stain that widens steadily as more and more ink is deposited in the center. However, it remains darkest at the center and gradually lightens as you move further from the center. This is a classic example of a chemical gradient.

One of the first growth factors involved in the repair phase of wound healing is the one found in platelets, the microscopic droids circulating in our blood that initiate clotting when a blood vessel is broken. Known as PDGF, or *platelet-derived growth factor*, this is a protein that causes certain cells to move and divide.

Now imagine you're a type of cell called a *fibroblast*. Part of your job is to be on the lookout for concentrations of the growth factor PDGF. As your day begins, you're resting calmly in your home tissue. This might be the fat layer under the skin, or connective tissue that holds everything together. Usually the day's activities involve eating and hanging out. Then the alarm sounds. Your receptors pick up the PDGF signal on one side of you, but not the other. This tells you to move in the direction of the highest concentration of PDGF—that is, toward the wound space. As you do, the ever-increasing chemical concentration of PDGF keeps drawing you further in. Eventually, once you're surrounded by a critical concentration of PDGF, that concentration tells you to start dividing. As you do, this creates an ever-increasing network of cells.

As the number of fibroblasts increases, they mature, stop multiplying, and start to produce collagen, the ropelike rebar that holds new tissue together.

How do you and your fellow fibroblasts know when to stop multiplying, start maturing, and start secreting collagen? It turns out that the local environment is the trigger.

Life in the wound space is anything but hospitable. It's an acidic, debris- and fluid-filled space with no oxygen. Bacteria thrive here. There is a transition zone in the wound space where enough oxygen and nutrients filter down from the surface to sustain some forms of life and not others. It's a zone of marginal existence and high stress. This transitional zone ranges from the last blood-filled capillary at the wound's edge to the area where there is so little oxygen that normal cellular metabolism cannot function.

Most cells use oxygen to create energy. (This process is called aerobic metabolism.) Most cells in our bodies have access to just the right amount of oxygen, so aerobic metabolism proceeds without difficulty. When the oxygen supply decreases, however, the cells can go into survival mode—a sort of cellular hibernation where they don't use oxygen anymore. This keeps each cell alive in difficult environments like the transition zone in the wound. One of the results of this survival metabolism, however, is the production of acid and a chemical called lactate. The high level of lactate in the wound space transition zone is the signal that tells fibroblasts to mature and produce collagen.

The chemical makeup of the material around each cell also tells it what to do. As fibroblasts move, divide, and secrete molecules such as collagen, they lay down a lattice of chemical messages that tell the cells that follow in their tracks what to do.

The low oxygen and high lactate levels in the wound space also tell the macrophages to produce and secrete growth factors that, in turn, tell the functioning capillaries at the wound edge to grow. This new capillary growth follows the movement and growth of fibroblasts by about twenty-four hours.

Each capillary is made from many single cells, called endothelial cells, linked together to form a tube. All the blood vessels in our body are also lined with endothelial cells. Our circulatory system is like a big tree, with our arteries getting progressively smaller as they get further from the heart. Capillaries are the smallest of these, like the tiny veins in leaves. The new capillaries that grow into this mesh of collagen and fibroblasts are like the plumbing system of a new building. They bring nutrients and oxygen to the growing and metabolizing cells and carry away waste products.

In normal, nonwounded tissue, capillaries rarely move, divide, or make more capillaries. However, the close proximity of a wound causes certain capillary cells to move toward the wound, divide, and make a new capillary loop. A different type of growth factor activates and regulates each part of this process. One tells the endothelial cells in the small veins at the wound's edge to contract. Another tells them to start to move toward the wound space. Yet another then tells them to divide and make more endothelial cells. A fourth growth factor tells the capillary cells to form a capillary tube. This then turns into a budlike structure and connects with others like it to create a capillary loop. Finally, blood starts to flow. In each new capillary loop, the junction between cells isn't tight, so blood cells and plasma can easily leak into the wound. As they mature, they tighten up their junctions where one cell connects with the next, and the leaking stops.

Nerves follow the capillaries into the newly formed tissue. Another group of specialized growth factors stimulates nerves to sprout new fibers and grow into the wound. At first, these new nerves are very excitable, making the wound sensitive to any disturbance or touch. As the tissue matures, however, the nerves also mature and become less sensitive. This explains why a new wound is very sensitive to any touch, but over time becomes less irritable.

This module of new tissue—led by fibroblasts that mature and form collagen, followed by new capillaries that provide oxygen and nutrients to the advancing tissue, and then nerves that provide communication with the rest of the nervous system—continues to grow until the wound space is filled. When the two edges of the wound grow together so there is no more wound space, this tells the macrophages in the wound to stop producing growth factors. Their job is completed; they can stand down. The hostile transition zone of oxygen, acid, and lactate is gone and the wound tissue is ready to be covered by skin.

Making New Skin

As tissue grows to fill the wound space, new skin gradually grows over the new fibroblast/collagen/capillary mesh.

To understand just how this works, it helps to know a little about your skin. Human skin has three different layers, each with a unique structure and function. The top layer is made largely of keratin, the same material found in fingernails and toenails. The upper layer of cells produces keratin in varying amounts, depending on the wear and tear on that part of the body. The more keratin, the tougher the tissue.

Calluses, which are formed as a response to superficial skin wounds, have more keratin than ordinary skin. If you chop wood for a long time, causing the axe handle to dig into your skin, your skin cells respond to the trauma by secreting more keratin to protect the skin from further damage. This creates a callus.

Below the keratin lies the epidermis, a layer of constantly replenishing skin cells that grow upward from the layer below. Sweat glands and hair follicles dot the epidermis at regular intervals, also extending up from the layer below.

The dermis is the deepest layer of the skin. The cells in this bottom layer constantly divide, and the new cells push up on the older cells. When the older cells get pushed further away from the blood supply of the dermis, they flatten out and start to produce keratin, just as the fibroblasts start to produce collagen when they move away from the blood supply at the edge of a wound. The dermis contains blood vessels, nerves, and supporting tissue, which provide strength and nourishment to the upper layers of skin. The blood vessels also remove wastes and act as a heating and cooling system for your body. By increasing the amount of blood flow through the capillaries, your body sheds heat in summer; by restricting blood flow in winter, it conserves heat. Sweat glands and hair follicles grow up out of the dermis.

When your skin is broken by a wound, the cells in the middle layer, at the junction of the epidermis and dermis, are the first to respond. Once new tissue containing fibroblasts, collagen, and capillaries starts to grow from the wound's edges, these active skin cells divide prodigiously, and then move over the newly formed tissue. Initially they are fragile and easily removed, so your body covers them with a scab, which is nothing more than a crust of protein. The new cells live in the protected area under the scab. They continue to divide and form a new epidermis.

This new skin produces lots of keratin at first, forming a callus over the new skin. Eventually the epidermal cells from both sides of the wound meet in the middle.

When the entire wound is covered with new skin cells, the scab separates from the most mature cells at the edge of the wound and falls off. Then a thick layer of keratin forms over the maturing skin cells as a protective coating. As the process of skin growth is completed, the keratin layer slowly returns to normal. Rebuilding is now complete and remodeling is ready to start.

The Remodeling Process

When you buy a home, you probably won't keep everything exactly the way it was when you first moved in. The same is true for new tissue filling a wound.

With wound healing, the process of remodeling begins immediately after the wound space is filled with tissue and new skin covers the surface. This process may go on for up to a year. At first, the changes are noticeable to the careful observer. Later, the changes slow down, so careful measurements or experiments are required to document the changes.

The first, most notable remodeling occurs in the size of the wound space and the blood supply. Once the wound space is completely filled with tissue, the process of contraction begins.

Let's take the viewpoint of a fibroblast once again. Remember, you're a cell that migrates from the cut edge of the wound and starts creating new tissue. As you divide, you secrete collagen, which connects you with other fibroblasts in a matrix. Now imagine you're at the wound's edge. All around you, cells are dividing and sending out ropes of collagen to knit your neighbors together. As you look back toward the edge of the wound and away from the wound space, you see new capillary buds growing quickly to supply needed nutrients and remove waste products. Looking in the opposite direction, you see the great abyss of the wound space, with macrophage soldiers cleaning up the last of the dead cells, bacteria, and foreign matter. They're also on their field phones, sending out growth factors to tell you which way to move.

As the wound slowly heals, you can see the fibroblasts on the other side of the canyon. Day by day, the canyon walls draw closer together. Eventually you move close enough to touch the other side. You anchor yourself to the opposite side with collagen. Growth factors order you to move and grow, so you do, exerting a pulling force that draws the two edges of the cut tissue together.

If the wound is small, contraction occurs and stops rather quickly, and the wound reduces in size only slightly. If the wound space is large, however, the process of contraction results in a significant reduction in the size of the wound. In loose-skinned animals such as mice, rabbits, and dogs, this process can reduce the size of a wound by as much as 90 percent. In tight-skinned animals such as human beings, the size reduction is typically about 30 percent.

The capillaries growing into the wound from its edge also change dramatically during remodeling. During certain stages of wound healing, the metabolic demands of the growing tissue are large. To supply sufficient nourishment, the capillary network becomes dense. New capillaries are formed, looped, and formed again, creating an advancing front of microscopic plumbing.

Once the wound space is filled, the frenzied activity quiets down to a more civilized pace. Contraction shrinks the wound space and the metabolic needs of the cells start to decline. In response, the number of capillaries starts to decline as well. Over weeks and then months, the decrease continues, eventually reaching a density that matches that of the tissue that was destroyed. As more time passes, the once-frantic cellular activity becomes a dormant scar.

This scar could be a thin line; a thick, hard ridge; a wide, shallow strip; or a large section of new skin only a few cells thick. It all depends on the extent of the wound.

Stop and Look

Take a few minutes to look your body over and find the scars that are reminders of wounds that have healed.

You now have a better understanding of the intricate process that resulted in each scar. I hope you also have a deeper appreciation for the miracle of wound healing.

CHAPTER 4

Psychological Wounding, Healing, and Development

Your psychological organism is as unique, complex, intricate, and robust—and, sometimes, as fragile—as your physical body. Also like your physical body, it is born with a built-in developmental pathway that will take many different twists and turns over your lifetime.

Your psychological organism—your psyche—consists of your ego or sense of self, your thoughts, and your emotional impulses and reactions. Included in these categories are your courage, your compassion, your hope, your gratitude, your fear, your outrage, your sense of justice, your love for others, and many other attitudes, values, and responses to the world.

Your psyche has a skin around it, just as your physical body does. This skin defines what's inside and what's outside, like a cell wall. It keeps out harmful energies and intentions, but lets emotional nourishment in.

This psychological skin is a living, changing, breathing entity that can be split and wounded. When this skin is broken, your psyche needs to heal. This healing requires energy, rebuilding, and remodeling, just as with your physical tissues. Like physical wounds, psychological wounding creates a space or void that needs to be filled and repaired. And if the psychological healing process fails, the consequences can be just as serious as those of a deep physical wound.

A healthy psychological skin is tough but pliable, and neither too thick nor too thin. It needs to be thick enough to keep out dangerous foreign bodies such as shame, blame, contempt, bias, and disrespect. But it also needs to be permeable enough to let in love, concern, support, appreciation, and other positive emotions and energies.

We all know people whose psychological skins are thin and brittle. Their egos are easily bruised and they are quick to take offense.

But a too-thick psychological skin can also be a problem. Many people who grow up in abusive or neglectful families grow thick, heavily callused psychological skins. As a result, they feel numb much of the time, and their capacity for intimacy, trust, and joy is greatly reduced.

As with your physical body, your psychological organism gets wounded in many small ways every day. A driver cuts you off in traffic; you take an embarrassing fall; a customer service representative is rude to you. We can usually heal these wounds easily, with a shrug or a curse or a deep breath. Larger wounds, however, often require plenty of energy, attention, and time to heal.

Psychological wounding causes very real, palpable pain. Recent brain function studies show that when someone we care about says something nasty to us, the words stimulate the same portion of our brain that responds to physical wounding.

You'll remember from Chapter 3 that physical wounds go through three successive stages of repair: 1) protecting the wound through inflammation, 2) filling in the wound and bringing its edges together, and 3) covering the healing wound with new skin or other tissue. Psychological repair follows a similar sequence of protecting, filling in, and covering.

However, there's one very significant difference between physical and psychological wounding and healing.

Our psyches are mostly about relationships—with other people; with groups such as families and neighborhoods; with pets or other animals we care about; and with God or a Higher Power. In addition to the psychological skin each of us grows around our sense of self, we also grow a relationship skin around each relationship we form.

We don't grow this skin on our own. We grow it with the person, group, or animal with whom we are in relationship. Keeping this shared skin healthy requires energy from everyone in the relationship.

The most obvious example is a mother and her child. While the child is still in the early stages of development in the mother's womb, there is no need for a relationship skin, because the mother's psychological skin completely envelops the fetus. However, when the child begins to develop a psychological skin of its own—after about three months in the womb—mother and child together grow a relationship skin that bonds them to each other. This skin stays in place throughout much or all of the child's life, until the mother or the child dies. However, in a healthy mother-child bond, this relationship skin changes significantly over time.

Every relationship we form creates such a shared skin. With close relatives, spouses, partners, and good friends, this skin is quite durable and solid. With less intimate relationships—coworkers, doctors, neighbors, etc.—the skin is much thinner.

Imagine that your best friend stands next to you. Now envision that each of you is surrounded by your own invisible, comfortable, close-fitting psychological skin.

Next, envision a large, clear bubble that comfortably and loosely surrounds both of you. That's your relationship skin.

Now imagine that you're standing with your immediate family. Each of you has your own psychological skin. However, you also share a larger relationship skin with each member of your family. And the family as a whole shares a still larger relationship skin, a bubble that surrounds all of you. (These images are all metaphorical, of course. Psychological and relationship skins are energetic and emotional, not physical or visible.)

Now imagine that one of your family members—your sister,

perhaps—says something that hurts you: "Sometimes you can act amazingly stupid and not realize it." Her comment cuts like a knife blade into both your psychological skin *and* the relationship skin the two of you share. You feel a pang of pain, and perhaps a flash of anger. You have been psychologically wounded—and so has your relationship. In both skins, a wound space has been created.

Then your sister shakes her head and says, "I'm sorry. I didn't say that very well. I didn't mean you personally. I meant that *anyone* can act stupid and not realize it. I meant 'you' in the general sense. You know, like 'you can't tell a book by its cover.'"

These words of apology and explanation quickly fill up the wound space in your and your sister's relationship skin. You feel forgiveness and understanding, which rapidly fill in the wound space in your own psychological skin. The pain in your psyche disappears. In a minute or so, both wounds are fully healed.

Now imagine that, instead of apologizing, your sister says, "I'm not saying you're a complete nincompoop—but you can be pretty obtuse sometimes. It makes me wonder how you made it through college."

These words deepen both wounds. Stunned, you consider your options and say, "I'm sorry you feel that way. I'm going home now. Maybe we'll talk later." You leave, and decide to sit under the tree in a nearby park for a few minutes.

As you relax, breathing the clean air and looking at the surrounding grass and flowers, you begin the process of psychological wound repair. This healing may take time and effort, and perhaps help from a friend or counselor or spiritual leader. It might involve ending, limiting, or redefining your relationship with your sister. Or it might involve having a discussion with her about what she said and how you felt about it.

Whatever you choose to do, however, you are the one with the power—and the responsibility—to heal your psychological wounds.

The wound in the relationship skin is another matter, however. That wound will remain unhealed unless *both of you* take steps to repair it. For your sister, this might mean apologizing, making amends, and promising to be more compassionate in the future. For you, it might mean listening to your sister's apology, accepting it, and forgiving her. Neither of you can heal the relationship wound on your own.

Healing a wounded relationship skin typically begins when one person says to the other (either overtly or by implication), "Our relationship is important to me. I want it to continue, and I don't want this wound to get in our way." If the other person responds in kind, healing begins immediately. If the other person doesn't, however, the relationship may end, and the relationship skin will wither and die.

There's one other difference worth noting between physical and psychological wounding: whenever a person inflicts a psychological wound on someone else, *they also wound themselves.*

Your Psychological Stem Cells

The psychological self begins its development in the womb, roughly three months after a sperm and an egg unite to create

an embryo. At this point the organs that sense the local environment begin to process inputs, and the developing brain starts to
remember what occurs. This creates the first psychological stem
cell: a rudimentary sense of self. Over the weeks, months, and
years that follow, this sense of self grows and differentiates, inter-
acting constantly with its surrounding environment. This enables
the psychological self to experience an ever-wider range of emotions and thoughts.

After about three months in the womb, a fetus's senses of hear-
ing, touch, sight, and smell begin to develop. The fetus senses the
mother's heartbeat and breathing. These create the beginnings of
psychological attachment and development. This mother-fetus
bond is every human being's first and most essential relationship.

The quality of the mother-child attachment affects the child's
psychological, physical, and mental development. Extensive studies show that the mother's attentiveness to her child's emotional
and physical needs creates the foundation on which that child's
subsequent relationships are built. The child's sense of security—
and, eventually, their personality—are closely related to the char-
acter and consistency of their maternal caregiver.

Normal brain development depends on this early attachment.
Severely deficient or abusive parenting can lead to problematic
structural changes in the way a child's brain processes information
and the way in which different parts of their brain communicate.

Once we are born, the development of our psychological selves
—our psyches—requires interaction with and attachment to other
psyches. This process of psychological differentiation progresses

in an ever-widening circle of relationships. Each new relationship develops its own dynamic that matures into a psychological entity with its own boundaries, sensitivities, characteristics, and life.

Over the years, our initial psychological stem cell—our earliest sense of self—eventually turns into the multiple selves that make up a human being: child, sibling, parent, community member, neighbor, friend, student, worker, lover, spouse, in-law, mentor, grandparent, etc. In a psychologically healthy person, the ability of the self to differentiate continues throughout life.

If we take good care of our psyches, we never run out of psychological stem cells, no matter how old we get. Our brain can continually create new neural pathways. Psychologically—and, as we will later see, physically and spiritually as well—a healthy person always has the capacity to change. This ability to remodel and reprogram is why good counseling and psychotherapy work. It's also why optimism and positive self-talk work to keep people healthy and happy.

A Tale of Psychological Wounding and Healing

So far in this chapter my examples of psychological wounding and healing have been quite simple. In practice, however, many parallel wounding and healing processes often take place at once.

As an example, let's look in on a family as a painful but common incident plays out. Lou and Maria are the divorced parents of two teenagers. Late one afternoon, both parents are sitting in Maria's living room, waiting for sixteen-year-old Rebecca to show up so she and her father can go to the gym together.

For the past three months, Rebecca has been infatuated with her first real love, Brian. Brian is a high school senior whom Rebecca met the previous summer; Rebecca is a junior. To Rebecca, Brian can do no wrong, though her father is lukewarm about him and her mother dislikes and distrusts him.

Rebecca walks in half an hour late, clearly distressed. Her eyes are red, her head bowed, and her shoulders bent forward.

"What happened?" ask her father and mother at the same time. Instinctively, her father holds out his arms in an invitation to a hug.

"Brian just broke up with me," Rebecca says softly, then starts to sob.

"Come here," her father says.

Rebecca sits on Lou's lap, puts her head on his shoulder, and nestles in his arms.

Lou holds Rebecca until she lets him know that she wants to separate by lifting her head and rotating away. She says "thanks," gets up, and sits on the floor by her mother's feet.

"I'm so sorry, honey," Maria says. "But, you know what? You're better off without him." She folds her arms in front of herself. "What did he say to you? What kind of excuse did he give you?"

Rebecca looks up at her mother. "He said he didn't love me as much as I loved him. And that it wouldn't be fair to me for us to stay together."

Maria snorts. "Well, girl, you learned something important about boys today."

"Mom, you don't understand. It wasn't a line. If you had been there and heard Brian—"

Maria cuts her off. "Oh, honey, I've been there dozens of times, believe me."

Loud footsteps echo from the kitchen. A moment later, Rebecca's thirteen-year-old brother, Edward, walks in. "Hey, Mom, guess what?" he half shouts—then stops when he sees his sister's face. "Yo, Chewbacca, what's up? Is something wrong?"

Rebecca glares at him, then leaps to her feet. "Leave me alone, you dork!" She runs to her bedroom and slams the door.

Edward looks at both his parents and asks, "Did something bad happen to her?" His father nods. Edward turns and shouts down the hall, "Okay, Sis, I'll be nice to you for forty-eight hours. . . ." He consults his watch. "Starting . . . *now*."

This incident illustrates the complex interactions that define our psychological selves, our relationship skins, and the interactions that can take place when psychological wounding occurs.

Rebecca is clearly wounded. Her relationship skin with Brian has been torn apart, and her own psychological skin has been cut. The tear in the relationship skin may or may not heal, depending on what she and Brian each do. But her psychological skin has been fairly deeply wounded by the sharp instrument of rejection. We commonly call this psychological wound a "broken heart" precisely because it goes deep.

Just as with physical trauma, this psychological wound sets off a cascade of physical and emotional responses. Initially it physically hurts; some of the same brain centers that are activated by physical trauma respond in the same way. That's why Rebecca cries, feels a bit faint, and eventually goes to her room and lies down. These are the same responses our nervous system would have to certain kinds of physical injury.

When Rebecca enters the living room, she is clearly in a psychologically wounded state. If this were a physical injury, she would need immediate medical attention; instead, because she is psychologically wounded, she needs immediate support, safety, and comfort.

When Lou holds out his arms to his daughter, he also extends the comfort and safety of the thick, resilient relationship skin that he and Rebecca share. She is reminded of the thousands of times she sat in his lap when she was young. Their relationship skin, which grew strong in those years, now encloses her and soothes her. As she nestles briefly in his arms, her awareness of that skin helps her begin to heal.

Rebecca and her mother share a similar relationship skin. When Rebecca sits by her mother's feet, she hopes to receive some additional comfort, safety, and empathy from her mother.

But when Maria was Rebecca's age, her eighteen-year-old boyfriend impregnated her, gave her herpes, dumped her for someone else, and moved to another state, all in the same month. Maria's own psychological wounds from those incidents have never fully healed. As a result, right now she can't bring herself to comfort her daughter with the thick relationship skin the two of them have developed together. Instead of reaching down and hugging Rebecca, she crosses her arms and bad-mouths boys. As Rebecca feels the sting of her fresh wound, Maria relives the sting of her own old, unhealed wound. For the moment, the relationship skin between mother and daughter becomes thin and strained.

When Edward comes in and sees his sister in distress, he shows some genuine concern—but he's a thirteen-year-old boy, so he also calls her a rude name. Like most siblings, he and Rebecca share a relationship skin that regularly thickens and thins. Psychologically, they're both used to helping each other heal in any given moment, and then lightly wounding each other the next. After Rebecca flees to her room, Edward offers her some support—and the comfort of their shared relationship skin. But he does so in classic adolescent boy fashion, by offering to treat her decently for two days. Though Rebecca will never say so to his face, she appreciates and feels slightly comforted by this gesture.

Psychological Infection

As we've seen, a wound space is created in any psychological or relationship wound, just as with a physical wound.

What fills up that space determines whether the wound heals or gets worse. When honesty, amends, and forgiveness fill up the wound space, the healing process is encouraged and supported. But when foreign bodies such as shame, vengeance, blame (including self-blame), or despair fill the space, they act like infections, slowing down or disrupting the healing process. When lots of these psychological bacteria get shoveled in, the wound may fester and become chronic.

People who were abused or neglected as kids usually grow up with chronic psychological difficulties. Their psychological wounds are full of foreign bodies that were imbedded over the years, creating constant inflammation and irritation. As these people grow older, they may—deliberately or unwittingly—continue the pattern of psychological wounding. This may involve re-inflicting or deepening their own old wounds, wounding others in the same way, or both.

Typically, in adulthood, these wounds need to be opened for them to drain and heal. This process is usually painful, but well worth the temporary pain. In some cases, what's dead and foreign—shame or blame, for example—also needs to be cleaned out.

Forgiveness

In later chapters in this book, we'll look more deeply into the process of psychological healing and how we can best support and sustain it.

In the meantime, please bear in mind that the most important element of psychological healing is forgiveness: forgiving the person or people who wounded you; forgiving yourself; and forgiving God.

CHAPTER 5

Spiritual Wounding, Healing, and Development

So far we have progressed from our relatively well-understood physical bodies to our somewhat-understood (and somewhat mysterious) psychological selves. In this chapter we'll look at our still more mysterious, and much less well-understood, spiritual selves.

The distinctions between these three selves are largely artificial, of course. Aboriginal humans saw no boundaries between body, mind, emotions, and soul. Only in the last few centuries has our understanding of the human organism splintered into three distinct areas of inquiry and knowledge.

Everything that lives is driven by an omnipresent life force. You can feel this force just by relaxing and paying attention to your body for a few moments. This force goes by various names and descriptions: *chi* (or *qi*); vital force; or, in Dylan Thomas's words, "the force that through the green fuse drives the flower."

This energy flows throughout our bodies, nourishing us. Well-documented, empirically proven therapies such as acupuncture and acupressure work to optimize this energy flow. Certain mystics and religious practitioners also seem to be able to tap into this flow, work with it, and direct it.

As yet we can't mechanically detect this energy or the pathways that carry it, but I'm willing to bet that some day—probably soon—MRI scanning will become sophisticated enough to pinpoint the flow of electrical impulses created by this force. Once we cross that technological threshold, we'll be able to map the pathways of this spiritual energy throughout our bodies. We may also be able to display computer-generated images of how our bodies are affected by spiritual thoughts, feelings, and experiences.

Spiritual Stem Cells

Spiritual development is as fundamental to human beings as the progression from a physical stem cell to an embryo, then a fetus, then a newborn, then a child, and eventually an adult.

As we saw in the previous chapter, we have psychological as well as physical stem cells. I believe that we have spiritual stem cells as well. These begin as nothing more than connections to this life force—a bit like nodes in a network or neurons in the brain. Ultimately, however, they grow into what we call a human soul, which both occupies and transcends our physical bodies and psyches.

Imagine this spiritual energy and its effects on the body and psyche as a continuum. On one end are the positive attributes of truth, love, justice, patience, tolerance, respect, moderation, and a discerning, reflective consciousness. At the other end are the negative attributes of hate, violence, dominance, excess, intolerance, greed, self-centeredness, and a generally unreflective consciousness. We can view the process of what we call spiritual growth as a progression toward the loving, positive end, and spiritual decline as a regression toward the negative end. (Note that this model is compatible with all the major religious traditions, as well as with humanism and other forms of compassionate agnosticism and atheism.)

For at least three millennia, there's been debate over whether spiritual growth is the project of a single lifetime or multiple lifetimes—and, if you accept the multiple-lifetime model, whether it starts and ends with humans, or starts with insects and progresses upward through reptiles and birds to lower mammals to humans. There's also, of course, the long-standing debate about how your location on the continuum determines what happens to you when you die. In this book I'm happy to leave these debates for others. Instead, I want to focus on what it means to grow, to be wounded, and to heal—spiritually, psychologically, and physically.

Let's look more closely at our spiritual stem cells. These contain the essence, instructions, and machinery to construct what we call our soul.

As with our physical bodies and psychological selves, each of us has a unique set of spiritual attributes that determines the makeup of our soul. This soul develops in synergy with our physical and psychological development. Over roughly twenty years, as we grow—first in the womb and then throughout our childhood—our physical, psychological, and spiritual stem cells grow and differentiate. Slowly but steadily, these three aspects of the human organism integrate to create a healthy adult, provided our development isn't disturbed by trauma.

As our spiritual stem cells divide, interact, and grow, they develop a maturing spiritual tissue that requires energy, nourishment, connections, and interactions. Nourish the soul and you progress toward the positive end of the continuum; deprive it of nourishment and it will regress toward the negative end. Our spiritual circulatory system strengthens and expands with use, and weakens and constricts with neglect, just like many parts of our physical body.

What many people overlook is that, to mature into healthy adulthood, *our spiritual selves also need stress, wounding, and healing.* Counterintuitive as this may sound, spiritual wounding and healing are as necessary to us as food, water, and air.

You'll recall from Chapter 2 that our adult stem cells provide us with new cells to replace those that wear out or die. In the proper environment, these multipotential cells can become almost any type of cell that our body needs. Adult stem cells thus continually allow us to reshape and resupply our tissues.

We have a similar pool of adult spiritual stem cells that allow us to reshape and revive our souls. These spiritual stem cells keep all the essential information that is needed to repair spiritual wounds and reconnect with our spiritual energy source. If our spiritual connection becomes diseased or damaged and the flow slows to a trickle, these spiritual stem cells usually survive in a dormant state, even though our spiritual faculties may starve, become ill, or die. Actions we take to restore the flow of spiritual energy will revive these cells and, with time and rehabilitation, a more normal spiritual flow can develop. The result is a rebirth of spiritual tissue and spiritual health.

Just as our physical tissues and stem cells require nutrition and waste removal to survive, our adult spiritual tissues and stem cells need nutrition and waste removal from our spiritual energy source (the *qi* or vital force). Lack of attention to our source of spiritual energy decreases our level of spiritual nutrition, while inattention to the health of our spiritual arteries, capillaries, and veins can diminish the delivery of this energy to the spiritual tissues in our soul.

In Chapter 3 we looked at how our physical arteries change to support the health and growth of tissue in our bodies. We also saw how certain diseases narrow our arteries or damage our veins, creating an increased risk for slow-healing wounds, and, eventually, cell death through tissue starvation. The same is true for spiritual illnesses and our spiritual arteries. Just like exercise, changes in diet, certain drugs, and reconstructive surgery are often needed to heal damaged physical arteries, we may need to heal and rehabilitate our spiritual arteries to restore the flow of spiritual nutrition and energy.

The Spiritual Lives of Three Women

Picture a small town square on Easter morning. On the west side of the square, surrounded by oak trees, is a church. The sun is shining; a gentle breeze blows the scent of apple blossoms in through the open windows. The church is full of neatly dressed families sitting in wooden pews, listening to the priest talk about Easter. Seated in the third row are two devout nuns dressed in their best habits.

The first nun sits with her back straight and her body relaxed. Her eyes are closed as she focuses on the priest's words and her own quiet breathing. The smell of apple blossoms fills her nostrils, her lungs, and her heart. Her whole body pulses with the renewing energy of spring, and her soul fills with the endless miracle of rebirth, renewal, and redemption. She is deeply at peace. As the spiritual energy flows through her, she senses the world being newly re-created, moment by moment. With each breath she renews her commitment to serving God and humanity.

Beside her sits another nun. She, too, sits straight and unmoving, but she is not relaxed. She looks at the fidgeting people in the pews with a cold stare of pity and contempt. To her they seem a collection of lost, pathetic, self-interested souls. She knows that most of them are destined for an eternity of fire. She shivers briefly, wishing she could do more than save her own soul and watch them rush to their own spiritual slaughter.

Outside the church, in a playground across the square, a young mother and her four-year-old daughter are playing. They chase each other, then roll down a small hill together, laughing and shouting. For a few moments they collapse on the grass together to catch their breath. Then they both jump up and run for the swings. "I get the blue swing!" the four-year-old shouts.

Let's look at the spiritual lives of the three adults in this scene.

The first nun, Sister Andrea, was raised by devout and loving parents who always encouraged her to take risks and try new things. When she was four, her parents brought her to the nursing home where they worked as volunteers, and from then on she felt a deep calling to serve others. As a teenager she showed great promise in the sciences, which to her revealed the awe-inspiring details of God's creation. By the time she graduated college, she knew her heart was in teaching the splendor of science to others; she also knew she could never turn her back on God. After a year of teaching math in a Catholic high school, she took the vows of a novice. Today she continues to teach high school science, and delights in being able to help teenagers wake up to the miracles of the natural world. Her life has been a generally steady movement toward the loving end of the spiritual continuum.

The woman seated beside her, Sister Angelica, is also a teacher in the nearby Catholic high school. She was raised by strict and abusive parents who put far more faith in rules than in love. Both were lawyers who told her throughout her childhood that they expected her to grow up to practice law as well. From the time she entered elementary school she was very tall and stocky, like her parents; as she matured, she was often teased for her size and shape. The one place where she felt safe and accepted was her church. In college she earned her degree and her teaching certificate as quickly as possible. Then—with great relief—she entered the convent, over her parents' angry objections. Today Sister Angelica is a strict disciplinarian with a black-and-white view of life and many unhealed psychological wounds from her childhood. The discipline and structure of the convent help her feel safe—but she is spiritually dying. Her spiritual arteries are tightly constricted, restricting the flow of spiritual energy to her soul.

Physically, Emily and Megan—the mother and daughter on the swings—resemble neither of the nuns. They're both dressed in brightly colored shirts and pants, and Mom has a parrot tattoo on her arm. Emily is a young single mother who made some foolish choices early in life and, as a result, has learned many tough life lessons. However, instead of seeking safety and seclusion, she went her own way, needing to learn things for herself, often through painful experience. This sometimes got her into trouble, but sometimes led her to great success. Today she has a thriving business as a commercial artist, and loves spending time with her daughter. Over the years, her spiritual stem cells responded to the wounds and challenges of life with greater questioning, smarter risk-taking, greater self-sufficiency, and more curiosity about the world. As she's matured, she's moved further and further toward the loving end of the spiritual continuum—sometimes by fits and starts, and with an occasional step backward.

Spiritual Arteriosclerosis

Injustice, hate, jealousy, abuse, and other negative emotions and actions wound our spiritual arteries and cause them to constrict. This is true whether we're on the giving *or* the receiving end of them. Continued wounding can shut off all energy flow, just as physical arteries can harden and close. The result is spiritual illness and, in extreme cases, spiritual death, where even the spiritual stem cells die.

History is full of people who experienced spiritual death while their bodies lived on. Some examples: Pol Pot, Adolf Hitler, Josef Stalin, Idi Amin, and Lucrezia Borgia. When this spiritual death occurs in a person with power over others, it results in severe hardship, agony, torture, and death for individuals, families, towns, cities, countries, and even societies. Fortunately, these cases are as rare as they are extreme.

Spiritual Rehabilitation

As a vascular surgeon, I've taken care of thousands of patients who had extensive, life-threatening operations. They usually spend the first day in the intensive care unit, where they have one nurse and extensive monitoring. Then, if all is going well, they are transferred to the "step-down" unit, where they are monitored a bit less closely and share a nurse with one or two other patients. When they stabilize, they are transferred to the surgical floor, where one nurse might take care of ten patients with the help of nursing aides. When they are ready to leave the hospital, I often suggest they spend two to six weeks in a rehabilitation facility, especially if they are elderly or fragile. At rehab they receive daily physical therapy, nutritional supplements, help with the activities of daily living, help with their medications, twenty-four-hour monitoring, and psychological support.

In cases of serious spiritual and psychological wounding or illness, a similar process of spiritual and psychological rehabilitation may be called for. Sometimes, sustained self-reflection in a safe and quiet place may be sufficient. More often, rehab requires the help of a friend, trusted family member, or wise professional. Sometimes the situation becomes so entangled, dark, and destructive that intensive work in a spiritual or psychological facility is required.

Let's look briefly at three examples of spiritual rehabilitation. We'll start with Emily, the single mom, then look at Sister Angelica, the disciplinarian nun, then at someone real rather than hypothetical.

Emily's rehabilitation story is a quite common one. She made good and bad choices in her life, but her natural resilience and drive generally kept her moving ever forward. However, after the birth of her child, the weight of this added responsibility and postpartum depression took away her energy and hope. As she sank deeper and deeper into despair, she finally realized that reaching out for help was her only sane alternative. Family wasn't available; she had no religious connections; and her local community was in a poor section of town, where community resources were scarce. But she did have a friend from her workplace, a commercial art and design studio. They talked occasionally by phone and sometimes had lunch together. At 10:00 PM one night Emily decided to call her. The phone rang and her friend answered the phone with a sleepy voice. Emily almost hung up, but caller ID had announced her identity. Her friend immediately said she was glad Emily had called. After some small talk, Emily choked up, started to cry, and told her friend that she needed help. Twenty minutes later the friend was at her front door. They stayed together all night, talked, cried, and eventually formulated a plan. It turned out her friend had been through a similar situation and had found real help in a women's group, and through the work of several spiritual writers.

Gradually, Emily learned how to manage her new life, with responsibilities as both a mother and a commercial artist. She joined a women's group, which gave her support and guided her path of discovery. In this group she slowly told her story, uncovered old spiritual and psychological wounds, and helped those wounds to heal.

As time progressed, Emily started to participate more and more in her group, and eventually teamed up with an older woman she really liked. This older woman had a similar history and had weathered the storm. She was wise, seasoned, and compassionate, and she wanted to give back to others who were in a similar situation. Eventually the two became strong friends. Emily's rehabilitation took time, but eventually she recovered her spiritual and psychological health.

Sister Angelica's spiritual rehabilitation story was quite different.

After she became a nun, she thrived in the structured and disciplined atmosphere at the convent. The daily ritual of prayers, song, and work gave her security and strength. She became a model of discipline and devotion. Then she was sent to teach seventh grade at the local Catholic school. Her quiet and regimented daily life was suddenly torn apart by six hours of challenges, five days a week. Her strict discipline was met with the equally strong opposing force of adolescence. To cope, she intensified her strict rules to the brink of brutality.

The school's principal, a nun from her same order, began receiving complaints from the parents of Sister Angelica's students. Eventually some parents threatened to remove their children from the school if Sister Angelica did not loosen her very tight grip.

Sister Angelica's rehabilitation took the form of an intervention from the parish priest, the head nun, and the school principal. She was given a two-month break from teaching to allow her to return to the convent, but she had to see the parish psychologist twice a week and join a small group of nuns with similar problems.

Her rehabilitation was tedious and challenging. She saw no reason to tolerate what she viewed as sinful behavior from her students. With time, however, the rehabilitation team showed her that her love of discipline and her strict interpretation of the scriptures were partly results of her childhood, and that love and tolerance were as important in the Christian life as discipline.

It took Sister Angelica over three years, but eventually she was able to rediscover her own deep love for God, for her fellow humans, and, especially, for her students. Today she still runs one of the stricter classrooms at the school, but she teaches with love, humility, and the occasional flash of humor. Not all of her students like her, but they all respect her—and she regularly receives letters from parents thanking her for inspiring her students.

Our third example of spiritual rehabilitation is my own story. I was the eldest male child in a very tightly controlled, conservative evangelical family. My grandfather was an elder of the church; my mother was the organist; and my father was a deacon. Each week we spent all of Sunday and every Wednesday night at church.

At home, however, I was sexually and physically abused. Although I was very intelligent, I did very poorly in elementary school, partly because of the abuse, partly because I was dyslexic and hyperactive, and I stuttered horribly.

Years later, as a young adult, my relationships with women were strained and very temporary because my social and sexual development had been stunted. I compensated by becoming physically strong and aggressive.

When I was twenty-five, I married an aspiring opera singer. But I soon developed an addiction to sexual relationships. I began an affair with one of my research nurses, left my first wife for her, and married her.

Then I discovered that my new wife had the same addiction I did—and a similar history of childhood abuse. I also learned that she had had multiple affairs of her own. We divorced as well.

Eventually I hit bottom. My life was a combination of a workaholic schedule, constant overeating, and one affair after another.

In despair, I took a month off from work and checked into a rehabilitation facility.

For a month, I spent 6:30 AM to 10:30 PM every day on one-to-one psychological therapy, writing, reading, exercise, healthy eating, group therapy, horse therapy, recreational therapy, and art therapy. For a month, professionals probed, explored, inspired, directed, challenged, and guided me. At the end of this month, we all agreed that I needed a second month of rehab. I agreed to another month of spiritual and psychological therapy in a less-intense facility.

Over time, meditation, walking, healthy eating, reading, resting, and inspiration from others opened my spiritual arteries and created new arteries around the blocks that had formed from years of disuse and abuse. I learned to appreciate the simple beauty of life, a source of spiritual energy, and the strength and guidance that come from a healthy spiritual connection.

Today I continue with regular psychotherapy, EMDR, meditation, walking, good nutrition, and helping others. In fact, this book is one of the biggest results of my spiritual rehabilitation.

CHAPTER 6

Why Wounds Are Good for You

Strange as it may sound, we all need wounds. They stimulate positive change, learning, and growth. They tell us what our body needs and teach us what's good and what's bad for us. They help us modify our behavior to support our health and healing.

Wounds force us to pay attention—and to change what we do —because they speak to us in elemental ways that other human beings can't. They force us to stop and take inventory of ourselves and what we're doing.

Wounds are wise taskmasters. They are also humbling, reminding us of our vulnerability. They demand that we honor our bodies, psyches, and spirits, treat them carefully, and not do anything stupid or dangerous with them.

It's fair to say that there are good wounds and bad wounds. A good wound—i.e., a small, nonchronic one—creates just enough stress to help us heal and grow, but doesn't create significant functional impairment. We incur good wounds from moderate exercise, yoga or stretching, deep tissue massage, serious (and respectful) debate, philosophical or spiritual inquiry, and honest self-examination. Good wounds strengthen and empower us.

In contrast, a bad wound creates so much stress that we can no longer function normally for some time. This is what happens when we sprain or break an ankle, when someone abuses or betrays us, or when we abuse or betray someone else.

Just before I began writing this chapter in the summer of 2010, I wounded myself badly. I was riding my all-terrain motorcycle too fast on a rough trail. I hit a bad bump and went down—and the dirt bike came down on top of me. The handlebar jammed into my eye; the hot exhaust landed on my leg, burning a deep hole into it; and many parts of my body got cut or scraped.

I'm sitting here now with a bandage wrapped tightly around my leg, looking at the thick scabs that show me I'm healing well. I've got a black eye that looks like I got in a bar fight. I'm also in pain—pain that tells me exactly when I need to stop walking, or go lie down, or take a nap.

A few days before my accident I was talking to my sister, who is a nurse. She said to me, "You're sixty-one years old. Why do you mess around on a dirt bike, especially at high speeds?" I told her, "Because it's fun." She said, "Sure, but it's also dangerous." I knew this as well as she did, of course, but our conversation didn't change my behavior.

My wounds did, though. No more dirt biking at speeds over 30 mph for me.

As I look at my own wounds, I can picture the many different messenger molecules flowing through my body, delivering a variety of messages. Each message is felt as a form of pain or discomfort. *Sit down. Don't bend that joint. Keep pressure off that leg. Don't touch this spot. Keep this area cool and dry.*

When a Wound Says, "Time Out!"

When you're seriously wounded—whether physically, psychologically, or spiritually—that wound supersedes almost everything else that goes on in your body. It redirects most of your energy toward healing that wound. It stops your digestion, keeps you from thinking very much, and stops you from complaining about the pain. The signal to heal is so strong that it will even let your muscles waste temporarily so that as much energy as possible can be redirected toward healing the wound.

We surgeons have a saying: *The wound masters all.* There's a good reason for this arrangement: if a big wound doesn't heal, you may die. By focusing so much energy and attention on a serious wound, your body may save your life.

If you get badly wounded, your body will produce a chemical called *cachexin* or *TNF*, a messenger molecule that carries a very powerful message. When cachexin is flowing through your bloodstream, all you want to do is lie down. You don't want to eat, or talk to people, or have fun. You just want to get horizontal and do nothing.

This isn't laziness or a lack of willpower. Your body is responding to a wound that's too serious to be ignored. It's saying to you, "Right now you need to stop what you're doing and focus on healing."

Only physical wounds produce cachexin. However, psychological and spiritual wounds can create a parallel response by reducing the production of serotonin in your brain. This reduced serotonin flow will also make you want to stop, lie down, and give yourself over to your own healing.

Clinical depression is a classic example of this. Depression makes you lie down and not be able to move or get up. Real depression isn't about feeling sad or blue. Your brain is producing significantly reduced amounts of serotonin. You've got a spiritual or psychological wound that your body wants to concentrate on healing—so it insists that you stop, lie down, and let its healing powers take over.

I had depression myself in 2001. I'm usually a very active person. I work hard and play hard. But over the course of a few days, I found it harder and harder to get out of bed and start working or playing. Eventually I could hardly move at all. Eating, bathing, and using the toilet seemed like Herculean tasks. I wasn't physically wounded, but I knew that my serotonin production was out of kilter.

After I spent a couple of days in bed, I knew my depression was serious. I made an appointment with a psychiatrist and said, in essence, "I've got a serious wound that needs to be treated. Please help me."

Like most serious wounds, my depression took some time to heal, and it required a variety of treatments: medication, talk therapy, and EMDR (eye movement desensitization and reprocessing, which I discussed briefly in Chapter 1).

Unless a wound is minor, stopping and resting is good for it. When you rest, your body can devote more of its energy to healing. As a result, you'll heal better and faster.

We all rest automatically when we're ill. But rest is just as important for moderate and serious wounds as it is for diseases.

Suppose that while you're cutting vegetables, you cut open your hand, and the gash is deep enough to need stitches. When you get home from urgent care or the emergency room, take a nap. Those two hours of sleep could shave a day or two off your healing.

The same is true of a nonphysical wound. Maybe your teenage son stays out all night, or you and your partner have a huge argument, or the promotion you were promised is unexpectedly awarded to the boss's son-in-law. Your psyche experiences each of these events as a wound, so treat it as such. As soon as you reasonably can, get some extra sleep. You'll heal faster.

When I'm under a great deal of stress for an extended period of time, I take a day off as soon as I can arrange it, and I just sleep. Usually I'm back to normal the following morning.

Most of us have taken an occasional day off from work when life threatens to overwhelm us. Although we may jokingly call these "mental health days," we're actually speaking the truth. If we spend those days simply resting, most of us will heal significantly faster from our wounds and be in better psychological and spiritual shape afterward.

Growth and Healing

In human beings—and in all living creatures—growth is a never-ending process. Our cells are constantly growing, dying, and being replaced by new ones. Our brains are always growing, too—learning new information and activities, creating new neural pathways in the process, and, as science has recently learned, growing new cells as well.

Unless we block the process, we steadily grow emotionally and spiritually as well—building new relationships; deepening existing ones; ending unhealthy ones; figuring out how to get along with other people; and learning how to connect more deeply with our Higher Power.

Like growth, healing is also never-ending. In fact, *growth and healing are variations of the same process.* Whether we're healing from a wound or growing from adolescence into adulthood, our bodies, minds, and spirits are building themselves up.

In biology, nothing changes without stress. In the absence of stress, living tissue stays exactly the same. After all, if everything seems fine, why change? It's only when tissue gets stressed in some way—when there's a change in pressure, or chemistry, or temperature—that tissue grows or heals. If you stress a cell—heat it up, or cool it down, or stretch it—that cell has to respond to the stress in some way. If it doesn't, it will die. So the cell either adapts to the stress by changing itself, or it reduces the stress by creating a change in its environment.

This is not only true for each of our cells; it's also true of all our organs and bodily systems. It's equally true for our ideas, beliefs, worldviews, and other psychic structures. And it's just as true for our relationships with other individuals, with our families, with all types of other groups, and with our Higher Power.

As we saw in Chapter 1, when we exercise or stretch, we lightly wound ourselves for our own benefit. Sometimes we also lightly wound ourselves to strengthen our relationship with another person. For example, because we're friends, you come with me to watch my daughter play soccer, even though it's so cold outside that your fingers feel numb. I come to your house to play poker once a month, even though I'm allergic to your three cats. We willingly suffer a bit, and do things we wouldn't ordinarily do, in order to be in each other's company.

Everyday Wounds

In a normal day, each of us gets wounded dozens of times.

When you shave, you lightly wound yourself with each stroke. You're not just cutting off the hairs; you're also scraping away the top layer of living tissue in your skin. That's why after you shave your skin is often sensitive—and, if you're light-skinned, it may temporarily turn pink. (Remember the first few times you shaved as an adolescent, and how raw your skin felt afterward? Over time, as you wounded yourself lightly in the same places over and over, your body adapted by growing tougher skin in those areas.)

When you sit in the same position for more than a few minutes, your butt or back begins to hurt. That's because it's become lightly wounded. The steady pressure on a few specific spots literally creates small wounds. Without thinking, you shift in your seat, removing the pressure from each wounded area. Your body then heals these tiny wounds within minutes. (If you don't adjust your position, these tiny wounds will grow into pressure sores within hours.)

If you do a lot of walking for your job, you lightly wound your feet every workday. After six or seven hours, the repeated pressure of each step mildly wounds some of your bones, muscles, ligaments, and tendons. That's why your feet hurt when you get home—and why they feel so much better when you elevate or massage them.

Throughout the day, all of us bump into things and scrape against objects, giving ourselves many tiny wounds. We give other people tiny physical wounds, too, when we hug them tightly, or shake their hands very firmly, or make vigorous and passionate love with them. (When you feel sore after sex, you're actually feeling a small wound.)

The list of common, everyday wounds goes on and on. Sunburn is a wound. Frostbite is a wound. Acne is a wound. A stiff neck is a wound. Blisters are wounds. Scratching creates tiny wounds. So does smoking. You even wound yourself while you sleep, just by lying in the same position for more than a few minutes. (This is why people in comas need their bodies turned regularly. If they aren't, they can develop serious wounds, called bedsores, just from lying in one position.)

We all regularly give ourselves light psychological wounds as well. After making a mistake, many of us say to ourselves, "Be more careful next time, you doofus" or "Okay, showoff, maybe now you've learned to ride your dirt bike more carefully." In psychologically healthy people, this isn't masochism; it's a way to help us pay closer attention. Like physical pain, this small, self-inflicted jab is a wake-up call that encourages us to change our behavior. We normally heal from these tiny psychological wounds in seconds.

We also regularly give *each other* small psychological wounds— sometimes inadvertently, sometimes deliberately. You buy Aunt Betty a cardigan sweater for her birthday, even though she specifically told you—nine years ago—that she hates cardigans. You forget a lunch date with an old friend. You tease your partner about his baggy pants. He teases you back about your Birkenstocks. You unwittingly embarrass your teenage daughter by asking her friends if they like Elton John. Then, because you see how mortified she is by the question, you put on your biggest smile and ask them if they like Three Dog Night.

Maturing as a human being means getting used to this inevitable, ongoing wounding. Our skin literally gets thicker and stronger in certain spots; our tolerance for physical pain increases, too. (As we get older, we also heal more slowly. Newborns heal from most small wounds in a day or two. Middle-aged adults take a few days to a week to heal from similar wounds. After the age of fifty, our healing time increases roughly 10 percent per decade.)

We also toughen up emotionally, and learn to shake off most minor psychological wounds. Yet we don't toughen up too much; we still stay open and vulnerable to other people we trust.

We all also regularly incur—and heal from—small spiritual wounds. Every time we hear about another human tragedy—an earthquake that buries thousands of people alive, a gunman who shoots a dozen school children, an innocent woman who is incarcerated and tortured to intimidate her family—we feel it as a spiritual slap in the face. When we're adolescents and young adults, these spiritual wounds may stun us and stop us in our tracks. As we get older, however—if our development is healthy—we learn to keep going in the face of such events, yet without numbing ourselves to them. We let ourselves be lightly wounded by each new tragedy; we pause for a moment, willingly suffer the spiritual pain of being human in this less-than-perfect world; and then we pick ourselves up and continue living our life with as much integrity as we can.

Resiliency

As each of us matures, we build our resiliency—our ability to recover from wounds of all types. Resiliency is crucial to our physical, emotional, and spiritual health.

If we grow up in a reasonably healthy family and society, we learn how to quickly heal from small wounds such as scrapes, shallow cuts, mild sunburn, everyday disappointments, small losses, and bad news. Our physical, psychological, and spiritual skins get thicker and stronger—but not too thick—in all the right places.

One of the benefits of regularly playing any competitive game, whether it's soccer or volleyball or chess, is that sometimes we lose. When we do, we feel disappointment—a small psychological wound. Over time, after enough losses, most of us develop the ability to quickly heal from disappointment, learn from our mistakes, and compete once again.

For years I coached my son's football team. Part of my job during training was to encourage players to wound themselves just enough. I would push them to the place where their hamstrings ached, because this meant their muscles were stretching farther and getting stronger. My goal was to get them to incur the optimum wounds and obtain the maximum gains.

I've seen second-rate coaches push players too far, to the point where they tore their hamstrings—thus incurring bad wounds instead of good ones. I've also seen mediocre coaches push their players too little.

It's exactly the same in the classroom and on the job. When I trained surgeons at the University of Minnesota Medical School, I would repeatedly push them to do their best. I'd show them new or alternative techniques, encourage them to be more careful or thorough, and ask them questions that forced them to think through the risks and ramifications of each decision. In the process, people's egos would sometimes get wounded a bit. But they would shake off the slight emotional pain, heal within minutes or hours, learn what they needed to learn, and become better surgeons as a result.

Indeed, any time we're pushed or challenged, we're being lightly wounded—and when we rise to that challenge, we heal and grow. This is the central dynamic of every human being's physical, psychological, and spiritual development.

CHAPTER 7

Healing a Wound Is Like Growing a Garden

When I was nine years old, growing up in south Chicago, I saw an ad on the back of a cereal box for atomic radishes. I'd never grown anything before, and we had no place to garden, but something about the name atomic radishes excited me. So I sent in a quarter, and a couple of weeks later a package of radish seeds arrived in the mail.

The only place I could find to plant the seeds was in a pile of cinders behind our house. Unpromising as that seemed, I tucked the seeds into the cinder pile, and every day I watered them. To my delight, after a week or so, radish shoots came up and grew strong and straight.

The vital force of life is so strong that these plants were able to grow in a pile of cinders in an alley. That same force of growth and healing lives in each of us.

Today, more than five decades later, I have a large vegetable garden and love to cook with foods from it. Yesterday, when my wife and I began our supper with tomatoes I'd picked from the vine only minutes before, I thought, *These are a gift from God.*

Here in Minnesota almost everyone gardens, and many people farm for a living. In fact, it was a Minnesota farmer who helped me see that healing a wound and growing a garden are similar processes.

The farmer, Gordon, was a diabetic who came to me with a nonhealing wound on the bottom of his right foot. After he told me the story of his wound and I examined his foot, I asked him, "Do you ever walk on this foot?"

"Sure," he said. "All the time."

"That's good news," I told him. "It means that if you stop walking on it for a few weeks, it will probably heal. Get yourself crutches, stay completely off it for five or six weeks, and the wound should disappear."

He shook his head. "Dr. Knighton, I'm a corn and soybean farmer. I can't stay off my foot for that long. There are things that need doing on my farm every day. Nature never goes on vacation, and I can't run my farm on one leg."

I could see that I wasn't going to convince Gordon with any of my standard wound-healing sound bites, so I said, "Gordon, when your corn is two inches tall, do you ever drive your tractor over it?"

"Hell, no," he said. "Why would I do that?"

"Well, what would happen if you *did* do that?

"I'd kill off half the corn."

I said, "Every time you step on your right foot, it's just like driving your tractor over young corn. You're wounding the same spot again and again, creating conditions that make it impossible for the wound to heal. Think about that the next time you step on that foot."

Gordon did stay off his right foot for the next six weeks. He swallowed some of his masculine pride and asked his kids and relatives to help on his farm. It turned out that they were happy to help—and they were thrilled to see him be a little less stubborn and a little more humble. Five weeks later, all of us were happy when his previously nonhealing wound healed completely.

What Every Physical Wound Needs to Heal

Growing a thriving garden—or a field of healthy corn—requires careful effort and attention. You need to:

- Create the right flow of water.
- Turn the soil (and then plant your seeds).
- Provide proper nutrients.
- Get rid of unwanted plants, animals, and objects.
- Protect plants from other types of damage.
- Do the right things at the right time.

All of these tasks form an integrated system. You have to do them all if you want an optimal harvest. You can't just give your plants enough water and sit back; weeds will take over, or wild creatures will eat much of your yield.

A wound needs all of these forms of attention and care, too, if it is to heal properly. Let's look more closely at each of these vital aspects of physical healing.

Blood Flow

Blood flow is as essential to a healing wound as water is to a growing plant. Indeed, proper blood flow is the key to healing, growth, and health.

When physical wounds heal slowly or not at all, poor blood flow is often the cause. Most treatments for slow-healing and nonhealing wounds thus involve improving blood flow. Increase the blood flow to a wound and it will almost always heal faster and better.

All our cells need water and nutrients (such as oxygen and glucose) to stay healthy. Wounded areas need considerably *more* water and nutrients to rebuild and replace damaged tissues. Blood is our body's irrigation system; it's how our cells get both nutrients and water.

The heightened biological activity in wounded areas also causes cells to produce more waste. Our blood removes these wastes and carries them to the liver, kidneys, and lungs for expulsion from the body. In people with poor blood flow, wastes can back up and become toxic.

If you've ever damaged a tendon or a piece of cartilage, you've learned from experience how important blood flow is. Tendons receive very little blood flow, so they heal very slowly. Cartilage receives no blood flow at all, which is why damaged cartilage almost never heals.

Our brains and retinas are just the opposite. They're made up mostly of capillaries—tiny blood vessels—because they need lots of nutrients to process the billions of signals that pass through them every day.

Many of the symptoms of diabetes are results of poor blood flow. Insufficient blood flow to the kidneys causes them to perform poorly and, sometimes, to cease functioning entirely. Poor blood flow to the retinas causes blindness. Poor blood flow to the hands and feet causes many of the nerves in them to die, in a condition called *neuropathy*. And poor blood flow keeps diabetics' wounds from healing.

Blood flow is also closely related to aging. Because a fetus in the womb is almost wall-to-wall capillaries, nearly every spot in its body gets superb blood flow. Scientists think this is why a wounded fetus can regenerate parts of its body—and why, when it heals, it doesn't scar.

As soon as we're born, though, our capillary density—and, thus, our blood flow—begin to slowly decrease. This decrease continues throughout our lives. By the time we're eighty or ninety, our skin may have so few capillaries that you can see through it—and when it's wounded, it can take a long time to heal.

Blood flow also helps to moderate our body temperatures. This is why elderly people are often more sensitive to heat and cold.

Adequate hydration is critical to effective blood flow. If your body becomes dehydrated, it shuts off the blood flow to certain tissues—first the fat beneath your skin, then your muscles, then your vital organs. Dehydration is the cause of many headaches, all hangovers, and feeling generally dragged out. It's also the main reason why people's bodies ache when they have a bad cold or the flu. Next time you catch a bug, try drinking two or three glasses of water instead of popping a couple of pills.

Plain water is the healthiest thing you can drink. Alcohol and highly caffeinated beverages *dehydrate* you, so when you drink those, drink plenty of plain water as well. I drink at least a gallon of water a day, but I'm 6'2", large boned, and physically active. A small man or average-size woman who spends most of their day in an office can usually stay well hydrated by drinking half a gallon daily.

Turning the Soil

To plant the healthiest garden, you don't just scatter seeds. You have to prepare the soil by tilling or plowing or digging. You need to change the shape and density of the soil so that each plant gets the optimum amount of water and nutrients.

When your blood flow is optimized, parts of your body change their shape as well: your arteries and capillaries literally expand, enabling them to carry more nutrients and water to every part of your body. Medical professionals call this process *vasodilation*.

The five tools for creating vasodilation are heat, exercise, mental activity, acupuncture, and massage. Here's what you need to know about each one:

Heat. Heat naturally causes blood vessels in your skin to expand; it also increases your heart rate. This is why so many health clubs have saunas.

Exercise. Physical exercise also increases your heart rate and generates heat, dilating your arteries and capillaries. Interestingly, even if you exercise only one part of your body, you'll still get improved blood flow from head to toe.

Mental activity. When you do puzzles, solve equations, learn a new language, study an unfamiliar subject, play chess, read philosophy, or simply think hard, you don't just sharpen your mind: you also fill your brain's arteries and capillaries with lots of blood. Creative activities—writing a poem, playing the piano, painting a portrait, or performing in a play—have the same effect. So does intense focusing, such as meditation or visualization. (Every time you learn or do something new, you also slightly change the physical shape of your brain in another way, by creating a new neural pathway in your cortex.)

Acupuncture. Although we still have much to learn about how and why acupuncture works, it appears to increase both blood and energy flow to certain parts of the body, expanding arteries and capillaries in the process. (Intriguingly, the opposite is also true: the stimulation of certain acupuncture points appears to *reduce* blood flow to parts of the brain, thus relieving pain.)

Massage. It's common knowledge that massage reduces stress, moves toxins out of tissues, feels good, and is deeply relaxing. Massage also improves your physical, psychological, and spiritual energy flows, and helps you reconnect to your body, your emotions, and your Higher Power. In addition, the healing touch of a caring human being, and the direct skin-to-skin contact, have a variety of psychological and spiritual benefits.

If you have a wound, however, the greatest value of massage is its ability to dramatically improve blood flow—even to parts of the body with no functioning arteries.

One of my first patients at the Wound Healing Institute was a blind massage therapist named Steve, who came to me with a large nonhealing wound on his shin. I tested the blood flow below his knee, and there was almost none. From the kneecap down, he didn't have a single functioning artery.

Back then, in the 1980s, we knew of no effective treatment for a leg in such bad condition. I told Steve, "I'm so sorry, but I don't know of a way to save your leg. We're going to have to amputate it below the knee."

Steve took a breath and said, "Doc, in my observation, massage increases blood flow. I think I can figure out how to massage my leg so that it maximizes that flow. Give me a few weeks to try that before you cut it off, okay?"

I said, "Of course—as long as you come in once a week and show me how your leg is doing."

Steve massaged his leg three times a day, and every week I measured its blood flow. Within two weeks, the flow had improved. Within seven, the leg had excellent blood flow, all the way down to the toes. Amazingly, because Steve's lower leg had no functioning arteries, all of this blood was being delivered through his capillaries. After eleven weeks, the leg wound had healed completely.

Now, some twenty years later, massage has become a standard part of wound healing. Twice a day for ten to twenty minutes is all that's needed. People can massage themselves, get massaged by a caring friend or relative or neighbor, or—the best option—go to a professional massage therapist. I'll provide more details about massage in Chapter 11.

There's one other way to increase blood flow: through surgery. When an artery or vein loses its ability to carry blood, it can often be surgically bypassed by grafting in a replacement artery or vein.

When we hear the word "bypass," we most often think of heart surgery, but bypass operations can be done almost everywhere on the body. I have done bypass surgery on hundreds of hands, arms, feet, and legs.

Another, more recent surgical treatment for improving blood flow is called *flap grafting*. This involves grafting in not merely an artery or vein, but a section of muscle or skin that contains many functional blood vessels.

Proper Nutrition

Every living thing needs nutrients to grow. Plants get it from the soil, and from the things we add to it (manure, compost, lime, commercial fertilizer, etc.) to maximize growth and improve yields. We humans get it mostly from the food we eat.

The best fertilizers are manure and compost, because they're unprocessed and ecological, and they contain everything most plants need to grow. Similarly, for us humans, the healthiest foods are whole and unprocessed. It's also important for us to avoid trans fats; to get sufficient protein; to eat enough calories to maintain healthy energy and blood sugar levels; and to get sufficient vitamins and minerals.

If you've got a physical wound, good nutrition becomes even more important. Pay particular attention to your protein intake; healing requires a lot of it. Also take extra vitamin A, vitamin C, vitamin D3, vitamin E, zinc, and omega-3 fatty acids. (I'll say more about these supplements, and suggest specific amounts to take, in Chapter 11.) If you're on a diet, check with your doctor; you may need to modify it, or even go off it, while you heal.

Just as gardeners add things to the soil, healers may include a variety of healing enhancements in their treatment plans. These include growth factors, hyperbaric oxygen, wound suction dressings, and several other options. These ancillary treatments have proven very effective, but they should be used only on the recommendation—and under the supervision—of a healing professional. I discuss these enhancements in Chapter 10.

Removal of Foreign Bodies

Any experienced gardener can tell you that what you remove from a garden is as important as what you put into it.

For starters, you need to get rid of anything in the soil that doesn't belong there—rocks, trash, tree stumps, branches, brush, and, especially, weeds. All of these foreign bodies can get in the way of your garden's growth.

Of course, you don't just weed once. You need to weed and clean a garden regularly, because new weeds keep shooting up, and new debris blows in. You also need to quickly get rid of any pests that take a liking to your plants.

Like gardens, physical wounds need to have foreign bodies removed if they are to heal. These can include objects, such as dirt, pebbles, bits of bone, and shrapnel; animal parasites, such as worms and insect larvae; dead or diseased tissue; pus and other unwanted fluids; and biofilm, which I'll say more about shortly. Any of these can infect a wound and prevent it from healing—or cause it to worsen and grow.

In wound healing, one of a surgeon's most important tasks is to thoroughly explore each wound and clean out all foreign bodies. Medical professionals call this process *debriding* or *debridement*— i.e., getting rid of all debris. This process is both an art and a science, because the inside of a wound is not always what it seems at first glance. Often an apparently small wound is actually large and deep—but most of the wound is hidden behind a thin layer of separating tissue.

A good surgeon explores each wound carefully, finding and testing its boundaries, and searches for such hidden or walled-off pockets. I usually do this by gently tapping the sides and bottom of each wound with a curette, a metal surgical instrument shaped like a tiny spoon. Literally hundreds of times, I've cleaned out what looked like all of a wound, then tapped its boundaries with a curette and discovered another pocket of infection underneath.

Countless patients have come to me with nonhealing wounds and said, "Dr. Knighton, I don't understand why this wound won't go away; my doctor cleaned it out, but it came right back." It usually turned out that their doctor only *thought* they had cleaned out the wound; in fact, they'd cleaned out only the uppermost section, and failed to discover other, hidden pockets. (Of course, it's important not to be too aggressive, either, or you will cut away healthy, living tissue.)

A wise surgeon also knows what fluids and tissues to send to the lab for testing. For example, patients often came to me with nonhealing wounds that had become infected with bacteria. Their doctors had prescribed antibiotics, which killed all the bacteria—but their wounds continued to grow. In each case, I opened, explored, and cleaned out the person's wound, but I also sent some of their diseased tissue to the lab, to check for a secondary fungal infection. Sure enough, as soon as the bacteria were gone, microscopic fungi had moved in and taken their place, substituting one type of infection for another.

One of the most challenging aspects of cleaning out a wound is biofilm, the slime that bacteria create when they adhere to a surface.

Scientists had very little understanding of biofilm until the turn of the millennium. Once we realized how biofilm functions, however, it completely changed how we think about healing.

Biofilm is almost everywhere. If you pick up a slimy rock from a stream, that slime is biofilm. The scum that grows on your shower curtain is biofilm. So is the gunk that grows in swimming pools and spas. Find a fountain in a nearby park; stick your fingers under the water and brush them against the bottom. That slipperyness you feel is also biofilm.

If you take a beaker and put water and some elemental nutrients in it—for example, if you spit or pee in it—bacteria will grow. Any source of sugar or protein will do. At first the bacteria will just float around in the water, where they are vulnerable to bacteria-destroying chemicals, but after a short time they'll adhere to the surface of the beaker and secrete biofilm.

The same thing happens inside your body. When bacteria first infect a wound, they can be easily destroyed by your internal defense forces—your macrophages, neutrophils, and white blood cells. But once they settle down onto tissue and secrete biofilm, that biofilm protects them from almost everything. This protective wall of biofilm is extremely difficult to penetrate. Even antibiotics can't get through. Bacteria thrive behind this wall in a sort of unicellular city, where they grow, divide, and infect living tissue. They also send off strands of biofilm to infect adjacent areas.

Biofilm is difficult to eradicate because it clings tightly to everything it touches. The molecules that form biofilm are long-chain sugar molecules, making it structurally like molasses. Trying to remove only biofilm is like leaving wallpaper on the wall while trying to remove the paste from behind it. A variety of chemicals can dissolve biofilm, but they also kill the tissue the biofilm clings to.

An infected chronic wound has biofilm all over it. We've learned, however, that when a wound is properly cleaned out— that is, when every foreign body or piece of dead tissue is identified and removed—the biofilm gets cleaned out as well.

By far the best way to deal with biofilm, though, is to treat wounds as quickly as possible, before bacteria have a chance to get inside, settle down, and begin the biofilm-secretion process. This is why it's so important to clean and bandage small physical wounds promptly, and to get equally prompt medical attention for larger ones.

Researchers have recently made some intriguing discoveries that may soon enable us to win the war against biofilm. A chemical in sphagnum moss appears to change the genetic makeup of bacteria, so that, instead of settling down and forming biofilm, they simply float about. In this state they can be easily killed by an antibiotic. If we can create a reliable treatment to render biofilm harmless in this manner, we will have defeated one of the biggest pests that can take up residence in a wound.

Protection

A garden also needs protection from birds, deer, rabbits, and other creatures that can eat or trample your plants. To keep them away, you may need to put up a fence, or a scarecrow, or a row of bells.

Your garden may also need protection from low temperatures —in which case you need to cover your plants on chilly nights to keep them from freezing.

You also need to protect your garden from your own carelessness. You're not likely to drive your tractor or dirt bike through it—but if you're not attentive, you may give it too much or too little water, or you may apply so much herbicide or lime that you sicken your plants.

While you're healing, your wound needs constant protection as well. Until a scab has formed, it needs to be covered with a dressing that should be changed at least once a day. It also requires your ongoing attention, to ensure that you don't thoughtlessly re-wound yourself by moving it or putting pressure on it.

Timing

In growing a garden, you don't just need to do the right things; you also need to do them at the right times and in the correct sequence. You wouldn't plant first and till second, or weed and fertilize your plants only after your harvest is complete. And here in Minnesota, you need to be careful not to plant too soon or too late. Do either one and you could lose your garden to frost.

Indeed, in gardening it's easy for one oversight or mistake to create a cascade of worsening problems. For example, if you wait a day too long to put up fencing around your tomatoes, rabbits may eat most of the young plants. So you put up the fence and plant new seeds, but these new plants are barely two inches tall when a hailstorm blows through town, killing most of the shoots. So you plant a third time, and get many hundreds of healthy, promising-looking tomatoes—all of which are killed by an early frost while you're away during the third weekend in September.

Timing is equally crucial in wound care. When you first get a moderate or serious wound, the sooner you can get to a healing professional, the better—and the more likely you are to keep the wound from getting worse. It's always easier—and less risky and expensive—to treat a small wound than a big one. Don't wait for the wound to become dangerously large.

It's just as important to see a healer promptly if a wound doesn't improve within two weeks. And if you're already under a healer's care and your wound is no better after two weeks, find a different healer and get a second opinion.

When you get a treatment plan from a healing professional, follow it carefully. Take medications, change dressings, and massage the area around your wound as the plan dictates. Don't modify it without your healer's approval.

Let's return for a moment to the tomato disaster, where one oversight led to a summer of wasted effort and a garden full of unripe, rotting tomatoes. Medical professionals call such a cascade of ever-worsening events a *negative feedback loop*. Each new event in this loop triggers a new, worse outcome.

Of course, in growing a garden, the worst outcome you're likely to suffer is an array of dead plants. But with a nonhealing wound, a negative feedback loop can lead to infection, illness, limb amputation, or even death.

Remember the woman from Chapter 1 who had a knot of undissolved suture sewn into her vagina? That knot became infected, creating great tenderness and sensitivity, as well as considerable pain. From that one event, a negative feedback loop began to form. The healers who examined her told her she was physically fine, and some suggested that the problem was stress. She *did* feel stressed, but that was only because she was in pain, her wound wouldn't heal, and she couldn't have sex with her husband.

Now let's suppose that, instead of coming to see me, she accepted the stress diagnosis, and she and her husband went to a marriage counselor. The counselor helped them improve their communication and encouraged them to cuddle more and to ease into sex more slowly and gently. Since none of this addressed the underlying problem, the woman's infection worsened and her pain increased. Soon even cuddling hurt.

The woman became more and more short-tempered. Her bewildered husband started spending more time at work and with his buddies. The couple began to argue, and sometimes shout at each other.

One day, as the woman fed her young baby, he kicked her lightly in the vagina. The pain was so intense that she screamed and dropped him on the carpeted floor. He wasn't hurt, but she worried that next time he would be. Her husband, who witnessed the incident, scooped up their son, held him against his shoulder, and asked her sharply, "Are you sure you're capable of being a mother?"

She began to wonder if she had a mental illness, and asked her friends to recommend a psychiatrist.

Before she could make an appointment, however, she began to run a high fever. She took acetaminophen, but it didn't help much. Finally, after five days, she went to urgent care. She discovered that she had serious sepsis resulting from a systemic infection, and was admitted to the hospital.

In this example of a negative feedback loop, doctors' initial error created a cascade of events and decisions that steadily worsened the woman's situation and compromised her health. What began as a small, localized infection turned into serious illness and a troubled marriage.

Fortunately, in real life, the woman came to me, and I was able to locate and fix the underlying cause. This replaced her negative feedback loop with a positive one, and she was able to heal.

Good healers are trained to look for negative feedback loops like this one. When they see one, their job is to identify the underlying problem, fix that problem, get the patient out of the negative loop, and replace it with a new, positive feedback loop.

What Psychological Wounds Need to Heal

Healing psychological wounds is also very much like growing a garden—and the same six basic gardening principles apply. Let's look at each of these principles through the lens of psychological healing.

Energy flow. In your psychological healing, the all-important flow is the flow of energy between you and other people who care about you. This means having trusted people in your life who will listen to you and provide you with empathy, support, and helpful feedback. It also means being able to say to these folks, *Would you help me, please? I can't do this on my own.* These people may include a talented psychotherapist, especially when a psychological wound is substantial or chronic. Support groups, including Twelve Step groups, can also encourage the strong flow of psychological energy.

Turning the soil. Self-reflection is essential to psychological health. If you simply react based on your initial feelings and impulses, you'll re-wound yourself repeatedly—and you may wound others as well. But if, instead, you carefully observe your thoughts, feelings, and impulses, evaluate them in light of their likely effects, and hold them up against your values, then you can act mindfully rather than impulsively.

Proper nutrition. Doing healthy things that please and relax you—creating art, playing music, gardening, fishing, or lying on the beach and watching the waves—can all provide psychological nutrition to help you heal.

Removal of foreign bodies. Removing foreign bodies is often the most important aspect of psychological healing. This process usually begins by determining where you end and where a foreign object begins. With psychological wounds, this isn't always as easy or obvious as it sounds.

Many of us had foreign bodies such as shame, distrust, cynicism, and fear of intimacy planted in us by others when we were young. As we grow older, we may get so used to them that we think of them as parts of us. But they're not. If these foreign bodies are not identified and removed, a psychological abscess can form around each one.

We didn't create these foreign bodies. They were passed on to us, like infectious diseases. But it *is* our responsibility to get rid of them. Until we do, we can't heal.

Psychological foreign bodies can also cause secondary infections. We imagine that we deserve our wound. We think we must have done something wrong. We believe we must be inherently flawed, or damaged, or worthless. These secondary infections also need to be explored and cleaned out.

The truth is that we *didn't* do anything wrong, and we're not inherently flawed, or worthless, or shameful. Somewhere in our past, someone else was unwilling or unable to heal from their own psychological wound. So, out of their own pain and fear, they wounded us and stuck a psychological foreign body inside us.

Secondary psychological infections abound. Often they take the form of unconscious self-talk. "I'm a victim." "It's always someone else's fault." "I'm a loser." "I'm special; normal ethics don't apply to me." "I'm unlovable." "If I let anyone see what I'm really like inside, they'll be appalled and go away." "I'll never find a decent partner." "I'll never forgive Mom for what she did." "I'm so screwed up." "I'm worthless." "I'm a bad person." "Men are all jerks." "Women are all bitches." "The business world is a jungle, so I'll make money however I can, and if I have to hurt someone in the process, so be it." "I don't have time to deal with this psychological healing crap." "I'm no wimp. I can just suck it up and keep going." "If I *don't* suck it up and just keep going, then I'm weak and pathetic." "The person who pushes the hardest and longest wins; that's how life works." These infections tend to create negative feedback loops—and habitual patterns of continued re-wounding—that harm individuals, relationships, groups, and, sometimes, entire communities.

Denial and psychological numbness are also common secondary infections. In trying to avoid the pain of our psychological wounds, we wall them off with a layer of psychological biofilm. Behind that biofilm, however, the original wounds grow and worsen. As a result, our capacity to care about others—and ourselves—becomes reduced. If we continue to try to avoid the pain, we may develop a third psychological infection: compulsive behavior or addiction.

Cleaning out psychological wounds begins with acknowledging that you're wounded. You then need to look at each wound clearly and honestly, and let yourself feel the pain it contains. Only after you have accepted and felt this temporary pain will you be able to remove all the foreign bodies. You can do this through emotional catharsis and release, or through a visualized rejection of the foreign body (*Here, Leslie, take back your damn cynicism. It's yours, not mine. I prefer to live a life of hope.*), or both. Psychological healers can be especially helpful with this process.

Psychological wounds don't just affect individuals; they also affect the relationships *between* people. This means that, for healing many psychological wounds, you have an additional option: you can go to the person who wounded you—or whom you wounded—and ask them to join you in the healing process.

We do this naturally when people we care about wound us in small ways. We immediately stop and discuss the situation with them honestly; we ask them questions; and sometimes we challenge them. Often this results in a quick apology and rapid healing.

The same process can also work with someone who has wounded you more seriously—but only *if* they are willing to participate in the healing process. (You can also heal on your own without their participation, but in such cases the healing won't be mutual.) Here again, a talented psychological healer can be enormously helpful.

Protection. You can protect yourself from being psychologically re-wounded by setting clear boundaries with other people, especially the ones who have wounded you in the past. This means being clear about what you will and won't allow them to do. It means saying no, and sometimes shouting, "Stop!" It can mean recognizing and leaving situations where you can easily be re-wounded. Sometimes it means ending or redefining an unhealthy relationship.

Timing. When we become psychologically wounded, we need to promptly make adjustments or ask for help. When a psychological wound is small, it's usually easy to heal it with a simple question or challenge or apology. But when it's not dealt with in a timely fashion, it may become infected and fester, requiring far more of our time, energy, and attention later on.

What Spiritual Wounds Need to Heal

You won't be surprised to learn that the same six principles for growing a garden also apply to healing spiritual wounds.

Energy flow. You can maintain a steady flow of spiritual energy by spending time in safe natural settings and by connecting to your Higher Power through meditation, prayer, yoga, or some other mindful activity. This connection includes asking your Higher Power for help and guidance when you need it—which, for most of us, is often.

Turning the soil. Spiritual healing differs from physical and psychological healing in one very important way. In healing physically and psychologically, we lean toward safety and security.

But in healing spiritually, we need to lean into the uncertain, the unknown, and, sometimes, the inexplicable.

Spiritual healing can take us in an unexpected direction or require us to sail into uncharted waters. It often demands that we let go of what we wanted or expected in order to follow an inner calling. That very calling may confuse or scare us at first—but following it will eventually transform us.

Most of us have narrow expectations for our Higher Power. We ask for guidance and help, yet we usually expect or hope for a particular answer. Then, when we get an answer that's different from what we wanted, we feel angry, resentful, or even betrayed. Part of our spiritual healing involves letting go of these feelings, and trusting a process that we cannot entirely explain or comprehend.

Proper nutrition. After you've asked for help and guidance, you also need to listen for that guidance, and be open to receiving it in whatever form or place it appears. This guidance can provide you with three forms of spiritual nourishment: direction, focus, and hope.

Merely listening to this guidance isn't enough, though. You also need to put it into practice in your life. If you don't act on the guidance you receive—or if you refuse to accept the guidance—your spiritual wound won't heal.

Removal of foreign bodies. Spiritual foreign bodies come in three basic forms: 1) despair or depression; 2) a sense that we are being punished by God; and 3) existential fear. This fear can manifest as a fear of change; a fear of God; a fear of the unknown, the uncertain, and the unfamiliar; or a fear of life itself.

Like other foreign bodies, these were implanted in us by others, usually when we were quite young. Typically, these foreign bodies create very painful, chronic spiritual wounds.

Sometimes a spiritual wound can be cleaned out through the simple, humble act of saying to your Higher Power, *I'm wounded and can't heal on my own. Please help me.*

More often, though, healing a spiritual wound requires the guidance of a qualified spiritual healer—a spiritual teacher, spiritual leader, or psychological healer with strong spiritual training and insight. Spiritual wounds can also be explored and cleaned out in spiritual retreats; in Twelve Step meetings; and in mind/body/spirit rehabilitation centers and programs. I'll say more about all of these in Chapter 10.

Protection. The protection of spiritual wounds is a paradox. On the one hand, we need to set and maintain clear boundaries with people who might spiritually wound us—especially spiritual leaders, teachers, and healers with deep wounds of their own. Yet we also need to stay open to inner guidance from a power greater than ourselves—and from people we trust and appreciate.

Timing. Whenever you get a spiritual wound, attend to it promptly, while it is still small. Spend more time in nature, in prayer, or in some meditative activity. If you need help or guidance from your Higher Power, ask for it promptly.

Also, as soon as you genuinely can, offer forgiveness—to the people who wounded you, to the human race, to your Higher Power, and to yourself.

It's an unfortunate fact of life that physical and psychological healing sometimes fail. We can maximize our healing response, but we can never guarantee that we will fully heal.

Spiritual healing is different. Genuine spiritual healing never fails. No matter what happens to our body and psyche, our spirit always has the power to heal.

Staying Alert

Suppose that one afternoon you notice an innocuous-looking vine growing at the edge of your garden. You don't think much of it, and soon forget about it. A week later, however, you notice it again—but this time it has reached into your bean patch. You're in a hurry, so you make a mental note to do something about the vine the next time you weed.

When you next check on the vine, five days later, it has climbed halfway up your beans. You realize the invading plant is kudzu, and you reach out to remove it. As you do, however, your cell phone rings. You answer it.

To your delight, it's an old friend you haven't seen in years. She's in town for a conference and wonders if you can join her for dinner in half an hour. You say yes and hurry inside to change your clothes.

When you get back to your garden two days later, after an enjoyable weekend with your friend, the beans are half shrouded in kudzu.

The worsening of wounds of all types can creep up on us like kudzu in a garden. Often, however, they progress much more slowly—and, thus, much more insidiously.

In my years at the wound healing clinic, I saw hundreds of patients with serious wounds that had grown slowly but steadily worse for months, and sometimes even years. Almost invariably, the wound began as nothing more than a slight, occasional pain or irritation. For example, someone might feel a minor ache in their leg after they walked several miles. At first, the person would shrug off the problem. As the months passed, however, the ache would appear after walking only three miles, then two, then one, then whenever the person walked anywhere. Eventually the pain would be present all the time; yet, because the wound had worsened so slowly and steadily, the patient had gotten used to it. In many cases, these patients came to me only after their spouses or partners insisted—or when the pain of their wounds finally became unbearable.

In healing as in gardening, it's important to watch for such subtle and gradual changes, and to address them as soon as they present a problem.

Small psychological wounds that worsen very gradually are especially insidious. For example, once winter begins, Alicia washes her hands often to help ward off colds and flu. When a new strain of swine flu makes its way across the country, she makes a point of washing her hands more often and more thoroughly. When she hears about the re-emergence of bird flu, she stops shaking people's hands, even though she knows that bird flu doesn't affect humans. After catching a bad cold, she stops touching everyone except her husband; she uses tissues to hold menus; and she uses credit cards instead of cash to avoid picking up germs from bills and change. What began as a reasonable health precaution has very slowly turned into a mild case of obsessive-compulsive disorder. Furthermore, Alice doesn't even realize it until her husband points it out.

Many neuroses, phobias, compulsions, addictions, and harmful habits begin in just this way—slowly, incrementally, and (if we're not being attentive) invisibly.

The same thing can and does often happen with spiritual wounds. Imagine that your coworker Sandy, whom you get along with well, tells a racist joke in a team meeting. You're startled because she's never demeaned any racial group before—but because everyone else laughs, and you want to stay on good terms with her, you simply sit quietly and impassively. Two weeks later, in another meeting, Sandy announces, "We've assembled a great team of dotheads in Karachi." No one else seems bothered by this—or even appears to notice anything strange about it—so once again you say nothing. Over time you stop registering these slights at work—until one day, as you're coaching an intern on an upcoming negotiation, you hear yourself say, "Stick to your guns; don't let him Jew you down on the price."

The slow, incremental worsening of wounds can also spill over from the physical to the psychological, the psychological to the spiritual, the spiritual to the physical, and so on.

A wound of any kind is an energy sink: it requires great amounts of physical, psychological, *and* spiritual energy to heal properly. Thus, when we're wounded, it's quite easy for our energy in any or all of these domains to become depleted. When that happens, and we don't or can't promptly replenish that energy, we can easily re-wound ourselves—and/or wound others.

Bart is grieving the sudden and unexpected loss of a friend, so he yells at his son for leaving the toilet seat up—and then mentally yells at himself for being a bad parent. On her way home from her physical therapy appointment, Tesilya trips and sprains her ankle; upset and exhausted, she skips her Al-Anon meeting, eats potato chips and cookies for supper, and tells a persistent telemarketer to screw himself. One Sunday morning, Rita's minister tells his congregation whom to vote for in the upcoming election. Afterward, in private, Rita challenges him and says that he's abusing his spiritual authority. He looks at her calmly and says, "Leave this church and don't come back; you're not welcome here." Shaken, she hits her head getting into her car and, a minute later, fails to see a crossing pedestrian, who leaps out of the way and then throws a rock at her car.

The effects of our unaddressed wounds can easily ripple outward, sometimes leading to a cascade of wounding and the creation of a negative feedback loop that can affect many different people.

The larger your sphere of influence, the wider such a loop can spread. In Bart's case, the wounding will likely go no further than his son—especially if Bart promptly apologizes and explains why he's upset. But Rita's minister has wounded, not only Rita, but many other people in his congregation. And if you're a public figure or other person with significant social influence, what you say or do can simultaneously wound hundreds, thousands, or even millions of people.

This is why it's so important to pay careful attention to our own behavior. If we are mindful, we can recognize when we have been wounded—and when we are about to wound others (or re-wound ourselves). We can then catch ourselves and stop the cascade of wounding, in much the same way that a gardener looks for, spots, and digs up weeds.

CHAPTER 8

The Miracle of Stem Cells

Stem cells are biological marvels—tiny but profound examples of nature's wizardry. They are also the key to many of the body's healing secrets.

Stem cells have already revolutionized how medical professionals think about wounds and healing. I believe they will engender many more such healing revolutions within the next ten to twenty years.

Let's take a brief look at what makes stem cells so marvelous— and so potentially useful in healing wounds of all types.

Stem Cell Discoveries

When a skin cell divides, it produces another skin cell. When a muscle cell divides, it produces a second muscle cell. Biologists call these kinds of self-replicating cells *differentiated cells*.

But stem cells are different. When a stem cell divides, it doesn't have to produce a new stem cell. If it's given the proper biochemical message, it can become many different types of cells.

All stem cells are not created equal, however. Some are considerably more malleable than others.

A *totipotent* stem cell can divide into any kind of cell in the human body: a brain cell, a fat cell, a blood cell, a liver cell, a muscle cell, a bone cell, another totipotent cell—anything. It's a cellular jack-of-all-trades. A totipotent cell can be identified by its unique set of affiliated proteins, which biologists call *markers*.

A *pluripotent* cell can also divide into a variety of different cells, but only those cells that make up a particular organ or tissue. For example, a bone marrow stem cell can become any kind of bone marrow cell (a red blood cell, a white blood cell, a platelet cell, a capillary cell, a fat cell, etc.), but it can't become a neuron or a liver cell or a tendon cell.

Each of us starts out as a single stem cell. When a human sperm and egg unite, they create an *embryonic stem cell*, or zygote. This quickly divides into two stem cells, then four, then eight, and soon tens of millions. Embyronic stem cells are totipotent: as they divide, they eventually become all the different types of cells in the human body.

But all human beings—not just embryos—produce stem cells. In fact, we now know that *adult stem cells*—sometimes called *somatic stem cells* or *adult peripheral stem cells*—exist almost everywhere in our bodies, including our brains and hearts. (Brain stem cells were discovered quite recently, in the mid-2000s.) Given the right conditions, these stem cells can divide into a range of different cell types, regenerating the relevant tissue or organ. But they're pluripotent, not totipotent. A lung stem cell can morph into different kinds of lung cells, but can't turn into a brain cell. This makes sense: why would you need brain cells in your lungs, or vice versa?

The term *adult stem cell* is used to differentiate it from an embryonic stem cell; it's inaccurate, though, because by the time you're born, all your stem cells are of the "adult" type.

Adult stem cells can be harvested harmlessly and almost painlessly from any healthy adult or child, and then applied to that person's wound to help it heal. In fact, adult stem cells are already being tested as a treatment for a variety of diseases and conditions, including autoimmune diseases, cerebral palsy, limb ischemia, degenerative joint disease, heart failure, type 2 diabetes, multiple sclerosis, osteoarthritis, rheumatoid arthritis, spinal injury, and certain eye diseases.

As of this writing, most forms of treatment using a person's own stem cells have not yet been approved for general use in the United States or Canada. However, many new treatments are being used on a limited basis in clinical trials.

Until very recently, scientists thought that there were only two types of stem cells: embryonic stem cells, which are totipotent, and adult stem cells, which are pluripotent.

Now, however, we know that there is a third type. Like adult stem cells, these cells can be harmlessly harvested from adults and children; like embryonic stem cells, however, they appear to be totipotent. They also have the same markers as embryonic stem cells. Intriguingly, these stem cells come from *inside wounds*. I and my colleague Vance Fiegel discovered these stem cells, which we call *wound-derived stem cells*, in 2009.

In the lab, wound-derived stem cells have turned into muscle cells, capillaries, neurons, tendons, and *osteoblasts* (or *osteoplasts*), the cells that produce bone. Tests are under way to make sure that wound-derived stem cells can become all the other types of cells that make up a human body. So far, all evidence points to their being able to do so.

Healing with Wound-Derived Stem Cells

When you become physically wounded, your wound begins producing large numbers of stem cells three days after you get your wound. The wound continues to produce these cells for another ten to twelve days, or until the wound is fully healed, whichever comes first.

Initially these stem cells divide and produce more stem cells. But when certain growth factors reach them, they are told to give birth to capillary cells, and, boom! you get capillaries galore. This is what normally happens in a healing wound.

We've discovered how to harvest and isolate these stem cells before they get this message. When the cells are put into a collagen gel and applied to a *different* wound, they don't grow into capillaries—they grow into whatever types of cells that wound needs to heal. This dramatically speeds up the healing process.

For example, in experiments done in my research lab, we cut rats' Achilles tendons, then applied a stem-cell-rich collagen gel to those tendons. Normally tendons heal very slowly because they receive very little blood. But the rats that were treated with wound-derived stem cells healed far faster.

A few years from now, if research and development continue on their current promising course, you'll be able to harvest and use your own wound-derived stem cells to help your wounds heal far more quickly. Here's what we envision:

You'll go to your doctor's office or clinic, where a medical professional will push a tiny mesh implant into the tissue under your skin, creating a very small, invisible wound. This will feel much like having an intravenous needle in your arm. After you wear this implant for a week to ten days, you'll return to the office or clinic, and the implant will be quickly and easily removed. The implant will now be full of many millions of wound-derived stem cells. If your wound is on the outside of your body, these stem cells will be added to a gel and applied to your wound. If your wound is internal, they will be mixed into a solution and injected into the appropriate spot. You won't have to worry about your body rejecting these cells, because their ancestors came from inside your own body. And, of course, no embryos will have been harmed in the process.

Stem Cells and Growth Factors

You'll recall from Chapter 3 that our bodies are teeming with thousands of different kinds of messenger molecules, which tell cells what to do. Each different type of messenger molecule carries a different message and triggers a unique cellular response.

Messenger molecules that tell cells to grow, move, and divide are called growth factors. When a growth factor called *bone morphogenic protein* encounters a wound-derived stem cell, that stem cell will give birth to osteoblasts, the cells that make bones. But if, instead, a growth factor called *nerve growth factor* encounters that same stem cell, the stem cell will create neurons.

Wound-derived stem cells can help any physical wound heal better and faster. But that wound can heal better and faster still when it is given just the right combination of wound-derived stem cells *and* growth factors. The two come from the patient's own body, and work together in a healing dance that is both exquisite and enormously efficient.

Research combining wound-derived stem cells and growth factors has just begun. But we already have some very good studies that show that a similar form of therapy, using a combination of adult stem cells and growth factors, helps hearts heal faster after they've been operated on.

Freezing Stem Cells

Stem cells of all types can be frozen indefinitely in a cryogenic bank, just as human sperm and eggs can. When these cells are properly thawed out, they come back to life, good as new. This means that your stem cells could be harvested and frozen at any time. When you incur a wound, these cells could then be quickly thawed out and applied to your wound to help it heal faster.

Growing Hearts in the Lab

What I'm about to tell you will sound like science fiction, but it's fact. Dr. Doris Taylor, a medical researcher at the University of Minnesota's Stem Cell Institute and its Center for Cardio-vascular Repair, has created functioning hearts in the laboratory using adult stem cells. As of this writing, she's created pig and rat hearts. By the time you read this, however, Dr. Taylor—or some-one else—may have created a fully functioning human heart in the laboratory.

Here's how the process works. Dr. Taylor begins with a dead heart from a deceased animal—in this example, a pig. She cleans it thoroughly, stripping it of all its cells. This leaves a lifeless matrix in the shape of a pig's heart—what Dr. Taylor calls a "ghost heart" or a "skeleton of a heart." She then injects this matrix with adult stem cells harvested from a live pig. These stem cells give birth to millions upon millions of heart muscle cells. These colonize the heart matrix, creating a new heart. Most amazing of all, on its own, *the heart begins beating*.

Tissue Engineering

Can the same sort of thing be done with human body parts? Yes. In fact, it's been done for years—though, as of this writing, not yet with a human heart.

Dr. Anthony Atala's research team at Wake Forest University has taken adult stem cells from people with faulty bladders and, in the lab, grown new, healthy bladders for them. The patients' dysfunctional bladders were then replaced with their healthy lab-grown counterparts. The Wake Forest research team is currently working to grow many other types of human tissue from stem cells, including heart valves, muscle cells, arteries, trachea, finger bones, and even ears.

Other scientists are doing similar work. Researchers at the University of Michigan have grown bone marrow from adult stem cells in the laboratory, and in 2009, scientists at Columbia University grew part of a human jawbone from adult stem cells.

As of this writing, organs and tissues grown in the lab have not received government approval for widespread use. But such approval does not appear to be far away. By 2011 or 2012, a custom-grown bladder, created in the lab from your own stem cells, may be available—with other stem-cell-grown tissues and organs to follow soon thereafter.

One added benefit of using people's own stem cells—both wound-derived stem cells and adult stem cells—is that they won't need immunosuppressant drugs to keep their bodies from rejecting replacement organs.

Stem Cells and Psychological Healing

Stem cells also play a crucial role in psychological healing. Using stem cells, the brain produces large numbers of new neurons every day. These do more than merely replace dead tissue.

Our brains also use them to lay down new neural networks—to rewire themselves.

Through this rewiring, our brains—and our psyches—are able to learn, grow, change, and heal. We can use these neurological tools to modify how we think, what we focus on, how we feel, and how we respond to a variety of situations. We can develop new habits and intentions and get rid of old ones. This is the case whether we're 5, 25, 65, or 105 years old.

Each time we deliberately change what we do or think, we begin to carve a new neural pathway into our cortex, using neurons produced by our brain's stem cells. The more we repeat that particular type of thought or action or intention, the deeper its related neural pathway becomes. Over time, repetition makes that pathway easier and easier to choose and access. This is how we develop new (and, ideally, more helpful) habits. And there is no end to the number of new neural pathways we can create.

We also have the opportunity to let go of habitual thoughts and actions that we don't want. Instead of passively following an old neural pathway, we can notice when we start to go down it, catch ourselves, and go down a different, healthier one instead— or create a brand-new one. When we stop using a certain neural pathway, it fades away over time, much like an unused path in the woods disappears under new growth.

The discovery of stem cells in the human brain has radically changed our view of psychological healing. A very few years ago, some types of psychological trauma, mental illness, and personality disorders were thought to be incurable. Now, however, researchers hypothesize that, given the proper conditions, the brain can heal from many forms of serious dysfunction using stem cells. Thus there is now great hope where previously there had been none—even for people who have suffered severe psychological trauma or abuse.

We know from PET scans and functional MRIs that the brains of many of these people have structural abnormalities. But neurologic and stem cell research now suggests that many of these wounds have the potential to be healed with good self-care, proper diet, the guidance of a talented psychological healer, and, in some cases, medication.

I don't mean to say that such healing is brief, simple, or painless. Often it is precisely the opposite. Indeed, my own healing from years of abuse has been long, complex, and often painful. But I am living proof that it is possible.

Furthermore, I was able to do a great deal of healing in only two months, during an initial period of intensive mind/body/spirit rehabilitation at Sierra Tucson, a psychiatric hospital and treatment facility in Arizona, and at Life Healing Center, a similar facility in Santa Fe, New Mexico. After only two months, I had etched many new, healthy neural pathways into my cortex. These were quite shallow after only two months, of course. But with attention and repetition over the years, these pathways have grown deeper day by day and month by month. (In the next chapter, I'll tell a story of how I healed from one incident of abuse by creating a new neural pathway.)

As we have seen, physical and psychological healing have many parallels. However, the growing of new neural networks reveals one crucial difference. When an otherwise healthy person sustains a physical wound and does nothing to re-wound themselves, the wound heals naturally, on its own. It may not heal optimally, but it will normally heal fully. When we sustain a significant psychological wound, however, our psyche does *not* heal itself automatically. For full healing to occur, *we must also decide that we want to heal—and we must take conscious steps to do so.* Often this involves getting help from a psychotherapist or other qualified healing professional.

Stem Cells and Spiritual Healing

We heal from physical wounds by growing new, healthy tissue. We heal from psychological wounds by creating new neural pathways. We heal from spiritual wounds, however, by growing new or deeper connections to something greater than ourselves—God, our Higher Power, our vital force, the Divine, Brahman, Ein Sof, or whatever else you want to call it.

In all three forms of healing, we regenerate parts of ourselves—but in spiritual healing, this regeneration includes both us and something larger than us.

As you'll recall from Chapter 5, each connection we have with a Higher Power is a kind of spiritual stem cell, offering us the opportunity to heal, grow, and regenerate in a variety of ways. These spiritual stem cells can morph inside us into many different wholesome characteristics: mindfulness, compassion, empathy, humility, understanding, generosity, patience, openness, clarity, equanimity, forgiveness, flexibility, and even wisdom. As we focus our attention on these spiritual connections through practices such as meditation, prayer, and contemplative solitude, we increase the flow of spiritual energy through our spiritual arteries. This energy strengthens our spiritual healing—and it can support our physical and psychological healing as well. There is even some preliminary evidence that connecting with a Higher Power increases the production of *physical* stem cells. Remember Dr. Taylor, the woman who grows new animal hearts in her lab? She and her colleague Richard Davidson, from the University of Wisconsin, took two blood samples from Matthieu Ricard, a Buddhist monk, a translator for the Dalai Lama, and the author of *Why Meditate?* and many other books. After they took the first blood sample, Ricard meditated for fifteen minutes; then Taylor and Davidson took a second sample. This sample showed a *huge* increase in the number of adult stem cells in Ricard's blood.

Did Ricard's fifteen minutes of meditation—i.e., the opening of his spiritual arteries—induce this healing response? Would anyone who meditated for fifteen minutes get the same results? Would thirty minutes of meditation produce even more stem cells—and how many more? Half again as many? Twice as many? Do forms of meditation other than the one Ricard practices yield similar results? Should wound healers recommend meditation as part of a standard healing regimen? I hope that we will soon have some good, research-based answers to these questions.

CHAPTER 9

The Healing Power of Reprocessing

I once operated on a patient who had a large, deep abscess that was filled with pus. After I drained out the pus, I explored the wound to find its boundaries. I went deeper and deeper, at times breaking through layers of dead tissue, and found more pockets of pus underneath. Finally, several inches down, I reached the bottom of the wound, where I found a small piece of infected bone. That one piece of bone had kept healthy tissue from growing, resulting in an enormous infected wound. And that wound would have kept growing until the bone fragment was removed.

I got rid of the fragment and cleaned out the wound thoroughly. Now, finally, this previously unhealable wound could heal. And it did: in about two months it was gone.

Physically healthy people rarely incur such deep and chronic physical wounds. When they do, however, those wounds are inevitably too painful to endure—and people quickly get themselves to healers for treatment.

Many of us have psychological or spiritual wounds that are equally deep and chronic—and equally problematic. Like physical wounds, these can't heal until they are fully explored and cleaned out. Yet we often force ourselves to live with these wounds rather than get them healed.

Sometimes these wounds are profoundly painful. Often, however, we wall them off or make ourselves numb to protect ourselves from the pain. Although this may help us get by in the short run, our wounds then grow and fester inside us, posing ever-greater risks to our psychological and spiritual health—and, sometimes, our physical health as well.

As you know, one big danger of diabetes is that it reduces blood flow, especially to the hands and feet. As a result, some nerve cells starve and die, creating a condition known as *neuropathy*. People with neuropathy literally can't feel parts of their bodies. Most of the nerves in those parts have died, so these areas become numb to pain, pressure, heat, and cold. Without normal sensory input from living nerves, people often re-wound those areas, creating a negative feedback loop that can lead to limb amputation—or even death.

When we cut ourselves off from our psychological and spiritual wounds, we create a similar negative feedback loop. Because we don't allow ourselves to feel the pain of our wounds, we may repeatedly re-wound ourselves—often in the same place and the same way. We find ourselves doing harmful or unhealthy things—yet we may have no idea why. Our wounds then get bigger and more serious, creating much misery for us—and, often, for others as well.

In such cases, we need to reverse the negative feedback loops. This begins by recognizing that we're wounded, acknowledging how much pain we're in, and getting ourselves to a skilled, trust-worthy healer.

As we saw in the previous chapter, deep, chronic wounds of the psyche and spirit *can* be healed. Sometimes, though, our most common healing tools—traditional talk therapy, art therapy, writing, spiritual counseling, meditation, prayer—can't go deep enough to fully explore and clean out these wounds. They may remove the top layer of dysfunctional psychological or spiritual tissue, but there may be much deeper, walled off, unseen pockets of infection underneath. We may think for a time that we've been healed—but, because the wound hasn't been fully cleaned out, our problems return.

To get at these wounds, a qualitatively different approach—one that involves revisiting and reprocessing traumatic events—may be necessary. This approach also needs to put our brain's stem cells to work, creating new neural pathways and building new habits of thought and action.

The therapeutic techniques for such deep healing don't involve wallowing in old memories, resentments, and hurts. Instead, they involve moving *beyond* the past. With the help of a qualified healer, we cut through our psychological and spiritual defenses and remove the foreign bodies from our psyches and spirits. Then, at last, we are able to heal.

Two healing techniques—one quite new and revolutionary, the other more familiar—enable us to reprocess and heal psychological and spiritual trauma in this way. The first, eye movement desensitization and reprocessing, or EMDR, was developed in the late 1980s. The second, therapeutic trance, has some commonalities with ordinary hypnosis, but is as different in its essence and application as a surgical glove is from a mitten.

Both EMDR and therapeutic trance are forms of psychological or spiritual surgery. However, both are noninvasive (i.e., they don't involve physical surgery or needles). Both require the guidance of a wise, compassionate, highly skilled healer. And both have proven profoundly effective. These forms of healing enabled me to explore, clean out, and heal from several large, painful wounds that had festered for decades.

In most cases, EMDR and therapeutic trance are used in addition to traditional talk therapy rather than in place of it. I'll provide an example of how the two work together later in this chapter.

EMDR and therapeutic trance often produce quick, positive results—sometimes after only two or three sessions. Like all forms of healing, however, they require full presence and honest commitment from the person who hopes to heal.

Both of these healing tools readjust our psychological and spiritual operating systems—which means they can do serious damage if they are misused. This is why they should be wielded only by a capable, caring, appropriately trained healer—usually a mental health professional. They shouldn't be used by an ordinary hypnotist, or by a minister or physician or psychotherapist who has not been carefully trained in their use, or by your friend who read about them in a book. They also shouldn't be used in groups, as a party game, or if you're drunk or high. You wouldn't ask your neighbor to open and drain an abscess in her garage because she just got her knives sharpened and lives only two houses away. Similarly, don't entrust your psychological and spiritual well-being to anyone who doesn't deserve that trust.

Let's look more closely at each of these tools for healing.

EMDR

EMDR is based on neurology—on how the brain processes information, experiences, and memories. It works with the body, the brain, *and* the psyche—and, sometimes, the spirit as well.

You're probably familiar with rapid eye movement (REM) sleep. During REM sleep, our eyes move quickly back and forth behind our eyelids, and we dream. It's a mentally active experience during which our brains process a great deal of internal information.

In EMDR, we do a similar kind of processing of past events—except that we are fully awake as we do it. We recalibrate our brain's basic operating and processing system so we can open mental doors we couldn't open in the past. (This is why some people say that EMDR takes them to a new and different psychological place.)

The physical aspect of EMDR involves repeatedly moving our attention from side to side, much as we move our eyes during REM sleep. Some people follow lights that flash alternately on their left and rights sides. Others keep their eyes closed and stationary, and instead follow a sound that alternates from ear to ear in a pair of earphones. Still others use handheld plastic tabs that vibrate like cell phones—first in the left hand, then the right. My own preference was a combination of earphones and vibrating tabs. This side-to-side movement of attention facilitates the transmission of information between the two sides of our brain. This helps us move past denial, numbness, mental blocks, and old psychological tapes.

But EMDR is not a purely mechanical process. Once you get used to the back-and-forth rhythm, your healer begins asking questions. *What are you feeling right now? What are you remembering? In your mind, where are you? What do you see, or hear, or smell? Who else is there with you? What's happening around you? How old are you?* Feeling their way, step by step, the healer takes you back into your own memories, some of which you may have access to for the first time. The process is partly a focused dialog, partly a therapeutic dance.

The healer's questions are neither haphazard nor standardized, but based on whatever your wound needs to be fully explored and cleaned out. Usually this begins with a problem or symptom. *Whenever I go on a date, I have a panic attack after an hour or two. I don't know why, but whenever I go to the dentist, I feel like I have bugs crawling all over me, and I want to run away screaming. I can't stop dreaming about the land mines in Baghdad and my two buddies who died when they drove over one. I keep reliving that afternoon when the minister had his way with me in his study, and then told me he would ruin my parents' reputations if I ever told anyone what he did.* The healer's questions about this symptom or problem help you identify, access, and explore its source.

EMDR requires great skill, insight, and empathy from the guiding healer—and great trust from the client. This trust typically takes time to build. I spent two years working with my own therapist before I was willing to let him lead me in an EMDR session.

A Story of Healing Through EMDR

For years, whenever I did regular talk therapy with my psychotherapist, I would get an intense pain on both sides of my head. It didn't feel like a tension headache; it was more like a person or object putting pressure on the sides of my head. The pain would last throughout the therapy session, and always went away very soon after I left the office.

As therapy became more comfortable for me, and many of my psychological and spiritual wounds healed, I expected the headache to go away. But it didn't—even after four years.

At that point my therapist said, "Whatever's going on with your head, I don't think talk therapy is going to heal it. We need to go deeper. This is a job for EMDR. Are you willing to use it to address this problem?" Because EMDR had already helped me access and clean out several other wounds, I quickly agreed.

What follows is a look at how EMDR helped me locate, explore, and clean out the underlying wound that caused my headache.

I sit in my therapist's office with my eyes closed, concentrating on the alternating *neet neet neet* in my ears and the back-and-forth vibrations in my hands. I breathe slowly and deeply, letting my body relax.

After a few minutes, the sounds and vibration recede into the background. Suddenly I break through into another time and place. It's like when I'm in an airplane at night, ascending through storm clouds, and I finally break free into calm, dark, open sky.

Except I'm not in the sky. It's dark, but it's hot.

Where are you? my therapist asks.

I'm underground, in a basement—the basement of the Chicago triplex I grew up in.

How old are you? my therapist asks.

I'm five years old, and I'm with my grandfather. We're standing in front of the furnace.

We heat the building with coal. My grandfather asked me to come down into the basement with him so we can clean out the clinkers from the boiler.

I love my grandfather, and I like helping him do chores. He's the one person I get along with really well, and he's the only family member who is always kind to me.

But my head hurts bad on both sides. The pressure is terrible—and it just gets worse and worse.

Suddenly I know why: my grandfather is holding my head and squeezing it.

What's your grandfather doing? my therapist asks.

He's making me suck on his penis.

How do you feel?

My grandfather is smiling and grunting. I feel good knowing that I can make him happy. But my head aches terribly.

Then, in a sudden blast, he comes in my mouth. I can't breathe. The taste is terrible. I start spitting.

What's happening now?

"Swallow it," my grandfather says. "Don't spit it out."

I swallow it, gasping and crying.

When he's done, my grandfather says, "David, you can't talk to anyone about this. This is our secret. Understand? It's important."

I nod, and he smiles.

For forty-six years I kept my grandfather's secret. I even kept it from myself. Now, finally, I've broken through the wall I built around the memory. I found and explored the wound.

Now I need to clean it out.

Put the adult David in the room, my therapist says. What do you want to say to your grandfather?

Suddenly I'm standing in the basement as my adult, 6'2" self. Now there are three of us in the room: five-year-old David, fifty-one-year-old David, and my grandfather.

I step in between the boy and the old man. I look him firmly in the eye. "Don't you ever do this again," I say. "You're betraying the most intense love you could have. You're a sick man, and you have no right to pass on your sickness to an innocent boy. It's not just your cum that you're making him swallow. You're also making him swallow your shame."

I pick up the boy and carry him out of the basement, up the stairs, and into the light. Then I break down sobbing.

In a rush, all the anguish, the terror, and the betrayal come out. I cry and shake and howl for several minutes, until all the painful feelings have drained from the wound.

Neet neet neet. I hear the alternating sounds and feel the vibration in my hands once again.

What is your Higher Power telling you? my therapist asks.

"He's telling me to give the shame back to my grandfather. It's his shame, not mine." I hold out my arms and open my hands. "Here, Granddad. Take it. It's yours. I'm not going to carry it around inside me like a fetus anymore."

I open my eyes. I'm slumped in my chair, covered with sweat. Gobs of spit are on my clothes, my shoes, and the rug beneath my feet. I'm utterly exhausted, but cleansed.

I can barely walk out of my therapist's office.

I already know from experience not to schedule any appointments after an EMDR session. I go home and sleep.

The wound has been thoroughly cleaned out. Now, at last, after forty-six years, it can heal.

And in the weeks that follow, it does.

Therapeutic Trance

Therapeutic trances are utterly unlike the trances that stage hypnotists induce (or appear to induce) in their volunteer subjects.

In a therapeutic trance, the healer never takes control of the client or tells them what to do. Nor does the client zone out or become compliant and sheeplike. They are fully awake and aware at all times—in fact, more aware than usual—and they can think and converse normally. Furthermore, after the session is over, they have a full memory of what took place.

Psychologists Adam and Joanne Crabtree offer this concise and eloquent description of therapeutic trance:

> In psychotherapy, trance states can be used to tap the client's inner wisdom about what is needed for healing and to mobilize the client's latent self-healing power. The relationship between client and therapist is important, not because the therapist has the answers or does the healing, but because the client's own healing resources can often best be accessed in rapport with a skilled guide.... Therapeutic trance shifts our focus from the outer world to the inner world, in that way making the inner mind accessible.
>
> By giving us access to the inner mind, therapeutic trance can help us become aware of forgotten memories. It can also give us the opportunity to solve present problems and envision future possibilities.

A therapeutic trance is relaxed and deeply meditative. Your heartbeat and breath slow down, your mind is focused, and your eyes are closed. Unlike EMDR, there is no back-and-forth stimulus—in fact, there is as little external stimulus as possible. The healer slowly guides the client into and through steadily deeper meditative states, then into a deeply relaxed, highly alert trance. A properly guided trance can thus go deeper than EMDR, and access more carefully protected psychological and spiritual wounds.

The mechanics of initiating a trance differ slightly from healer to healer and client to client. Typically, the client lies down in a relaxed and comfortable position and closes their eyes. At the healer's direction, they begin following their breath in and out for a few minutes, until their metabolism slows and their focus becomes internal. The healer may then lead the client in a body scan, in which the client slowly moves their attention from the top of their head to the soles of their feet (or vice versa). As they move, they note the physical and emotional sensations in each spot, and tell the healer when they feel anything unusual.

When the healer senses that the client is ready, they guide the client with questions, as in EMDR. *Where are you now? How old are you? How old do you feel? What would you do now, as an adult, in this situation?* Also as in EMDR, they may offer suggestions to help the client clean out their wound. *Now put your adult self in the room. What do you need to say to each person?*

A trusting healer-client relationship is as essential to therapeutic trances as it is to EMDR. I didn't trust my own therapist with trance work until I'd done EMDR with him for two years.

The Wisdom of Reprocessing

These reprocessing techniques are deeply valuable in two other ways. First, as we learn to reprocess past events with wisdom and courage, we train ourselves to respond to *present* events with those same qualities. Second, reprocessing trains us to ask good questions—and to ask for help—in the present.

None of this happens suddenly or quickly. As with learning any new activity, we need to practice it, over and over—and we need to pay careful attention as we do. We deepen certain neural pathways as we travel and retravel them. Over time, processing and questioning gradually become integrated into our lives.

When I first began consciously practicing these activities, I had to stop, go to a place where I could be alone for a few minutes, and focus very deliberately on doing them. But after a few months of practice, they began to come naturally and easily—like gratitude or prayer.

Now, whenever I feel stressed or in psychological pain, I automatically stop what I'm doing and take a few deep breaths. Then I ask myself, *What do I feel right now? What does this feeling remind me of? How old do I feel? What impulse do I have? What do I need right now? What would an adult do in this situation?*

And when I'm lost or confused or stuck, I try to put myself in the same open mental state I experience in EMDR and therapeutic trance. Then I ask for help. Sometimes it's from another person. More often it's from my Higher Power, and the request is silent and simple: *Please help me.* If I don't even know whom to ask, I say to my Higher Power, *Please help me—tell me whom to ask.* Then I listen.

Sometimes I get a clear answer through an idea or insight. Sometimes I get an image, or a feeling, or an intuition. Sometimes events that occur soon afterward give me guidance. Sometimes I don't get an immediate answer, but I feel that I will later. Sometimes I get the sense that being lost or confused or stuck is exactly what I need to experience right now. And sometimes a voice in my head says, "You need to figure this one out yourself."

Although I can provide a hundred personal examples of such situations, here's one that involves life and death. I was in the operating room, repairing a terrible aneurysm on an elderly woman. The artery was so diseased and old that, no matter what I did, it kept falling apart. Eventually I had tried every surgical trick and technique I knew, but I still couldn't fix it. I stood there over the patient, not knowing what to do.

My anesthesiologist said, "Dr. Knighton, we really need to get ahead of this bleeding. If we don't, we're going to lose her."

I took a few deep breaths and calmed myself. Then I did what I often do in EMDR and trances. I said silently to my Higher Power, *I need help*. And I was quiet.

Suddenly I had a flash of an idea. It was a surgical technique I'd never used—or even thought to use—with an aneurysm before, though I'd used it occasionally in other kinds of surgery. I had no idea if it would work on such a damaged artery. But the woman on the table was only minutes from death.

I took another deep breath and announced what I planned to do. I leaned forward, put my hands back inside the patient, and tried the technique.

It worked. I repaired the artery and the patient survived.

Sometimes asking for help is all we can do—and often it's enough.

CHAPTER 10

Recent Breakthroughs in Healing

This chapter looks briefly at some of the most important recent developments in physical, psychological, and spiritual healing.

Two of the biggest such breakthroughs—eye movement desensitization and reprocessing (EMDR) and the discovery of adult stem cells—are discussed in detail in earlier chapters, so I won't go into them here.

It's important to understand that different kinds of wounds require different types of therapy. Please don't call up your local hospital and say, "I'd like to arrange for some hyperbaric oxygen therapy and some electrical bone stimulation." Because each wound and each patient is unique, any treatment needs to be chosen in close consultation with an appropriate healing professional.

Nevertheless, all of the breakthroughs included in this chapter are built on the time-tested basics of the science of healing. They are not mere fads or promising ideas, but techniques and approaches that have already helped large numbers of people to heal.

Everything in this chapter is intended as a quick, general introduction, not a detailed guide. To learn more, consult a qualified healing professional and/or the web.

Breakthroughs in Physical Healing

Most of us will never need—or even encounter—any of the following healing tools. But if you incur a serious physical wound, one or more of these treatments could save a limb—or even your life.

All of these healing approaches share the same goal: to restore the normal structure and function of your body's tissues.

Hyperbaric Oxygen Therapy

Hyperbaric simply means "high pressure." For many years high-pressure air has been used with deep-sea divers, to keep them from getting sick when they return to the surface after diving in deep water. They climb into a decompression chamber filled with air that is two to three times normal pressure; then, slowly, the air pressure is reduced until it is close to normal.

In the late 1960s, military doctors discovered that wounds heal faster in a high-pressure, high-oxygen environment. A few years later, experiments by Dr. Tom Hunt at the University of California–San Francisco Medical Center showed how important oxygen is to wound healing and infection control. I did three years of wound-healing research with Tom, and we discovered that if you deliver more oxygen to the body, wounds heal faster and better. In fact, oxygen is as helpful to healing a wound as taking an antibiotic. Neutrophils—the body's Marines—need oxygen in order to destroy bacteria. When your neutrophils have access to more oxygen, they do a better job of killing these bacterial invaders and securing the wound space.

In the late 1970s, researchers started combining high pressure with high oxygen. They put a patient in a pressurized chamber and had them breathe pure oxygen through a mask for two hours a day. The result: the patient's wounds healed even faster than they did with oxygen but no high pressure. Eventually they discovered that when you breathe highly pressurized oxygen, you increase the oxygen-carrying capacity of your blood many times over; as a result, more oxygen gets to your wounds. (Interestingly, surrounding a wound with pure oxygen doesn't help at all. Researchers tried this and discovered that you have to breathe the oxygen.)

In the mid-1980s, hyperbaric oxygen became a widely used wound care therapy. Today, we have one-person hyperbaric oxygen chambers that look like high-tech tanning beds.

Growth Factors

You'll recall that these are molecules that carry messages from cell to cell throughout your body, telling them what to do to heal. To fully heal a wound, many different types of these molecules need to work together.

In the early 1970s, researchers identified a handful of growth factors. Soon afterward I discovered several others, and in the decades that followed, my fellow researchers discovered many more. There may yet be hundreds of others that we haven't identified.

Growth factors occur naturally in our bodies—but research has shown that wounds heal much faster when certain ones are added to a wound in just the right amounts and combinations. When these are combined with the patient's own stem cells, their healing speeds up even further.

In the late 1970s, while doing wound-healing research, I developed a way to isolate and remove certain growth factors from blood platelets. At the time, I had patients at San Francisco's Veterans Administration Medical Center whose wounds wouldn't heal. So, after getting the required permissions, I drew a small amount of each man's blood, isolated his growth factors, and applied some of these additional molecules on his wound each day, embedded in every new dressing. The result: the vets' previously nonhealing wounds healed completely in a few weeks. That's how the topical application of growth factors began.

Today, growth factors are widely used in wound healing, orthopedic surgery, neurosurgery, dermatology, and many other medical situations. They are also often used in combination with hyperbaric oxygen therapy to create an ideal healing environment.

Extremity Pumps

Many wounds on people's arms and legs don't heal because the blood flow to or from their limbs is inadequate.

As you know, regular massage can greatly improve the blood flow to any part of your body. But you can improve the flow to an arm or leg even more by using an extremity pump. This is a device that squeezes your arm or leg at regular intervals, driving more blood into it (in which case it's called an arterial pump) or out of it, back to your heart (in which case it's called a venous pump).

The technology behind extremity pumps is similar to that of the automatic blood pressure machines you see in drugstores and gyms. You sit down, wrap your arm or leg in a piece of flexible plastic, set the pressure, and relax for half an hour to an hour. During that time the plastic fills with air and squeezes your arm or leg at regular intervals, much like a second heart.

Electrical Stimulation of Bone Fractures

When most people get a bone fracture, it's a crack, similar to one in a windshield—or the Liberty Bell. But some bone fractures are full breaks, like when you break a cracker in half. The bone is literally in two (or more) separate pieces. If the bone gets properly set, but it doesn't heal correctly with normal medical attention, we call the break a *nonunion bone fracture.*

Researchers have discovered that if you put an electrode in this type of fracture and send a small but carefully calibrated current through it, new bone forms around part of the electrode. This helps the broken bone to heal better and faster. The process—

sometimes called *capacitive coupling*—is painless, and the technology is fairly simple.

Originally this electrode was put on the end of a needle, which was injected through the skin and into the bone, next to the break. The electrode was connected to a 9-volt battery, and the patient would wear a needle/electrode/battery apparatus. Today this form of treatment is still available, but now we can also stimulate bone healing without needles, using electromagnetism. You sit down, put your arm or leg in a metallic cast, and relax for an hour or so while a machine shoots current into the wound without touching it. It's a bit like a tiny MRI machine or PET scanner.

Suction Dressings for Wounds

Wounds need to be drained, kept clean, and, in most cases, protected by dressings. In the late 1980s, researchers discovered that if you apply suction to a wound that's draining, it heals much more quickly. Today suction dressings are widely used for large wounds.

A suction dressing rests lightly on a wound and creates a vacuum around it. Until very recently, suction dressings used electric motors that rhythmically sucked out fluid and debris. In 2010, however, a hand-powered suction dressing was developed. It uses a small, simple cylinder with accordion-like folds, which is squeezed to create suction. It's light and portable, and costs just a few dollars, making it practical and easy to use for almost anyone with a draining wound.

Flotation Beds, Mattresses, and Cushions

You'll recall from Chapter 6 that sitting or lying in the same position for more than a few minutes can wound you. If you don't move, pressure sores form in the spots where your body rests on the surface beneath it. These sores can easily occur in people in comas, paraplegics and quadriplegics, and people with diabetes, nerve injuries, multiple sclerosis, or collagen vascular disease.

A flotation bed, mattress, or cushion helps prevent these sores. You don't sink into a flotation bed as you would into a mattress, futon, or waterbed; instead, you literally float on its surface. In one common design, the bed is a large bag filled partly with compressed air, partly with plastic microspheres the size of grains of sand. A pump circulates the air, keeping the microspheres in constant motion. When you lie on this bed, you're supported in thousands of different spots by the microspheres, all of which are steadily moving. You won't get a pressure sore because the entire bed is always moving slightly beneath you. Other designs of flotation beds combine air, water, and/or foam to achieve similar results.

Today you can get a flotation mattress overlay that goes on top of a standard mattress, box spring, futon, or waterbed. You can also get a small flotation cushion to put under your buttocks or feet.

Breakthroughs in Spiritual Healing

Both of the breakthroughs described below come in a wide variety of forms, and each has saved people's lives.

Spiritual Retreats for Everyday People

For many centuries, spiritual leaders, monks, nuns, and mystics have gone on spiritual retreat—either alone, in the wilderness, or in small, secluded spiritual communities. In these retreats, they left behind the day-to-day world for a week, a month, a year, or even longer, during which they focused on prayer, meditation, and other forms of communion with a Higher Power.

Generally, folks like you and me were not welcome at these intensive retreats. However, mainstream churches, synagogues, and mosques did offer us less formal, less intensive getaways, usually lasting a day or a weekend.

In the past few years, though, the number and variety of intensive spiritual retreats open to laypeople has exploded. Many of these involve silence and strict, almost monastic-like schedules. Still more notably, many are open to people from any spiritual tradition, not just members of a single faith.

These retreats take us away from the innumerable distractions of everyday life and improve the signal-to-noise ratio in our spiritual lives. We can thus listen more closely to our inner voices, focus on what's at our cores, and heal.

Each year, many hundreds of these retreats are available to anyone who wants to deepen their spiritual healing. Typically these retreats last between two and seven days, but they can be as long as several months. Most are for individuals, though some are designed for couples or families.

Many retreats focus on specific topics, such as shame or compassion or loving communication or meaningful vocation. However, many are more general spiritual getaways that include meditation, prayer, singing or chanting, study, yoga, time in nature, and/ or other forms of spiritual connection.

Many such retreats are offered by formal religious groups. Increasingly, however, spiritual retreats are also being offered by wellness centers, hospitals, health centers, addiction recovery groups and centers, and colleges and universities. The University of Massachusetts Medical School, for example, operates the Center for Mindfulness in Medicine, Health Care, and Society, which regularly offers spiritual (or, as the university bills them, mindfulness) retreats.

Today there are also retreat centers that enable people to create their own private spiritual retreats. One such spot, located a two-hour drive from my home, is The Dwelling in the Woods, "a place to focus on renewing your spirit, mind and body." Meals are provided, but there are no formal gatherings or programs. People become temporary hermits living in quiet solitude, in cozy, modern cottages. The folks who do retreats here are not monks or nuns, but doctors, electricians, business owners, teachers, and homemakers.

Nonreligious Spirituality

For two centuries, we Americans talked regularly about religion, but rarely spoke of spirituality. We defined ourselves as Methodists, Baptists, Roman Catholics, Jews, atheists, agnostics, and so on. When most of us needed spiritual healing or guidance, we went to our minister or priest or rabbi.

Then, not long ago, more and more people stopped aligning themselves with one religious tradition. "I'm ecumenical." "I'm open to all the mystical traditions." "I'm a Jewish Buddhist." At the same time, many congregations and religious groups began recognizing the healing power of practices from other traditions, and adopted or adapted some of those practices for their members.

These changes reflect a lessening need for group identity and a deepening interest in spiritual practices that have legitimate healing properties, no matter what their origins. Many people now focus on the power of *spirituality*—rather than the power of religion—to help them heal their spiritual, psychological, and physical wounds.

Nonreligious spirituality has no dogma, no specific beliefs, no judgment, no right or wrong way, no group inclusion or exclusion. It's simply a recognition of connection, relationship, and a vital force that permeates everything, every person, and every place.

To become part of a religion, you need to join or convert, and you need to accept certain precepts and follow particular rules. But nonreligious spirituality is available to everyone, everywhere, at any time—and you don't have to pass any tests of belief or orthodoxy to access it.

Breakthroughs in Holistic Mind/Body/Spirit Healing

Both of the breakthroughs described below can profoundly support physical, psychological, and spiritual healing. Each comes in many different forms and configurations. Some of these variations are overtly religious; some are spiritual and ecumenical; and some are secular, but with spiritual nuances or highlights.

Specialized Twelve Step Programs

The Twelve Steps are a set of guiding principles that support people's healing and recovery from addiction. They are not a formal treatment program, a religion, a code of ethics, or a form of psychotherapy. However, it is fair to say that Twelve Step groups are psychological and spiritual wound healing centers. (As we saw in Chapter 7, addictions are forms of nonhealing psychological and spiritual wounds.)

Although people have healed from addiction through a variety of approaches, Twelve Step groups have by far the highest rate of success. Researchers found that recovering addicts who attend Twelve Step groups are more likely to stay clean and sober than those who don't. People in Twelve Step groups also experience fewer addictive symptoms; need to be hospitalized or sent to rehab or detox less often; generally lead happier lives; and tend to live longer. The Twelve Steps have thus been called one of the most important public health advances of the twentieth century.

The first Twelve Step program, Alcoholics Anonymous, dates back to the 1930s. In the 1950s, two other Twelve Step programs were established: Al-Anon, for family members and friends of alcoholics, and Narcotics Anonymous, for people with drug addictions. More recently, a wide variety of specialized Twelve Step programs have emerged. These include Cocaine Anonymous, Marijuana Anonymous, Crystal Meth Anonymous, Heroin

Anonymous, Overeaters Anonymous, Food Addicts Anonymous, Food Addicts in Recovery Anonymous, Eating Disorders Anonymous, Anorexics and Bulimics Anonymous, Gamblers Anonymous, Shopaholics Anonymous, Debtors Anonymous, Sex Addicts Anonymous, Sexaholics Anonymous, Sex and Love Addicts Anonymous, Workaholics Anonymous, Online Gamers Anonymous, Exercise Addicts Anonymous, and Self Sabotagers Anonymous. Other Twelve Steps groups serve the families and friends of people with addictions: Alateen (for young family members and friends of alcoholics), Adult Children of Alcoholics (also known as Adult Children Anonymous), and Co-Dependents Anonymous, for family and friends of folks with addictions of any kind. There are also Twelve Step groups for people with addictions and mental illnesses. These go by the names Dual Recovery Anonymous and Double Trouble in Recovery.

Twelve Step groups have been essential parts of my own recovery from food addiction and sex addiction—and from the many emotional and spiritual wounds that these addictions covered up. I can personally attest to the immense wound-healing power of the Twelve Steps.

Mind/Body/Spirit Rehabilitation

People with combined body/mind/spirit wounds such as addictions, compulsive behaviors, posttraumatic stress disorder, depression, bipolar disorder, anxiety and panic disorders, obsessive-compulsive disorder, and eating disorders now have options for intensive healing that were virtually unknown a generation ago. These forms of intensive mind/body/spirit rehab help people with serious (and often multiple) wounds to quickly clean out those wounds, begin to heal, and learn to act in ways that will discourage their re-wounding. A month in residential mind/body/spirit rehab is said to be the equivalent of ten years of once-a-week psychotherapy.

The monthlong residential program I attended in 2004 at Sierra Tucson is a typical example of this type of rehab. (In fact, the Sierra model is used by many healing professionals and treatment facilities.) The program brings together multiple forms of healing: healthy eating, massage, sufficient sleep, detoxification, exercise, EMDR, Twelve Step work, group psychotherapy, individual psychotherapy, psychodrama, family therapy, horse therapy, art therapy, wall-climbing, writing, reading, communication skills training, and many more healing modalities.

As with many mind/body/spirit rehab programs, every day at Sierra Tucson is carefully structured; my planned activities began at 6:30 AM and ended at 10:30 PM. Everyone is in an enclosed 160-acre compound, cut off from the rest of the world and closely supervised. No alcohol, drugs, caffeine, personal computers, cell phones, sex, or masturbation is permitted. It's a combination hospital, jail, and boot camp—and it works.

It doesn't work for everyone, of course—some people can't handle it and quit, while others break the rules and get kicked out. But when many people finish rehab, they have turned many of the negative feedback loops in their lives into positive ones. They are able to return to the world with cleaned-out wounds, renewed hope, and the tools and skills to fully heal.

These rehab programs typically last about a month; most require people to live on site in treatment facilities. However, shorter, less comprehensive, and less ambitious—though still helpful—programs are also available. Often called *intensives*, these typically last five to ten days; some allow people to commute from their homes.

Like rehabilitation from a serious physical injury, mind/body/spirit rehab is difficult, painful, and very, very good for you. Also like physical rehab, it can yield fast and profoundly positive results.

CHAPTER 11

Simple, Effective Strategies to Help Yourself Heal

There are dozens of simple things each of us can do to optimize our physical, psychological, and spiritual healing. This chapter briefly reviews each one.

As you'll observe yet again in most of these strategies, strong blood and energy flows are the essence of healing.

Physical Healing

What you do and don't do about a physical wound can make a profound difference in how fast and how well it heals. I recommend that you photocopy the next few pages and keep them in your first aid or emergency kit, so that if you do become wounded, the guidance you need will be at hand.

Don't touch your wound. Don't pick at a wound, blister, or scab. Let it heal naturally. (However, if a blister gets red and painful around the edges, it may be infected. In this case, don't pop it; see a doctor.) Once a wound has fully healed, it's okay to touch it—but do so gently and judiciously during the first few days.

Cover the wound with a dressing or bandage until a scab begins to form. All the standard types and brands of bandages work well. Be sure to change the dressing at least once a day.

Never skip changing a dressing because it hurts. This will slow the healing process and could infect the wound.

If your wound requires steady drainage, check with your doctor; you may need a suction dressing.

Keep the wound clean. Before you put on a new dressing, rinse the wound thoroughly with plain water or sterile saline solution. The water temperature doesn't matter—whatever feels good. Once you can see that the wound is healing, you can use a little soap, if you want—but be sure to rinse it out before putting on the new dressing.

Don't put anything on a wound except a dressing; water or sterile saline solution (when you wash the wound); and aloe, zinc oxide, or petroleum jelly. Many "healing" creams, gels, soaps, and ointments—including some regularly prescribed or recommended by doctors—don't help wounds heal at all. In fact, some can actually interfere with healing by drying out your wound, killing many of its live cells, or inducing an allergic reaction. Only a few over-the-counter preparations genuinely do help. Petroleum jelly protects and soothes wounds; creams, gels, and ointments made of aloe or zinc oxide support the body's healing process.

(Aloe is naturally derived from a common succulent.)

Keep the skin around wounds moist—but not wet. Optimum healing occurs when the intact skin around a wound is as normal and healthy as possible. To keep this skin properly moist, apply a bit of petroleum jelly; or Eucerin cream; or arnica cream, ointment, or gel. I especially recommend arnica, which inhibits excessive inflammation. (Arnica is naturally derived from a plant in the sunflower family.) Other salves and lotions can be expensive; some people have allergic reactions to them; and "healing" lotions can evaporate quickly, sometimes drying out the wound.

As much as possible, keep recently wounded areas from moving. Movement can reopen and worsen a wound. It can also create a large, thick scar once the wound finally heals. This is why healers often immobilize wounds on or around joints.

Don't put pressure on a healing wound. If you have a wound on the bottom of your foot, don't walk on it. Use crutches or a wheelchair until the wound has *completely* healed.

Regularly massage the area around a wound—but not the wound itself. You can do this yourself for ten to twenty minutes, two or three times a day; you can have someone who cares about you do it for you; or you can go to a good massage therapist. (Ask your doctor to write a prescription for massage; most are happy to, and many insurers and HMOs will cover massage when it's prescribed by an M.D. or osteopath.)

If you massage your own wound, put a small amount of massage oil or vegetable oil on your skin (not on the wound itself) in a radius of about eight to ten inches away from the wound. Your skin should be slightly slippery, but not dripping. Apply moderate pressure—enough to work the muscles and surrounding tissues, but not enough to cause pain. Move slowly toward the wound, then away from it, in a repeating pattern. Listen to your body—if the massage hurts, you're too close to the wound; if it feels good, you've found the right spot.

If your wound is very recent, you may need to wait a few days before beginning to massage the area around it.

In the first 24 hours after you become wounded, avoid all over-the-counter pain medications except acetaminophen (commonly known as Tylenol). Acetaminophen does nothing but relieve pain, which is why it's fine for most people to take it at any time. But aspirin, ibuprofen, Aleve, Anacin, Bufferin, Excedrin, and many other over-the-counter pills reduce both pain *and* inflammation. You'll remember from this book's early chapters that inflammation is a necessary part of the body's initial healing response to being physically wounded. If you take one of these drugs, it will inhibit many of your body's early messages that tell a wound to heal. After twenty-four hours, however, the initial healing response is complete, so from this point on, these drugs are fine—and even recommended if the area around your wound is inflamed. (By the way, when you do take acetaminophen, *never* take more than the recommended or prescribed daily dose; if you do, you can seriously damage your liver. And if you routinely drink more than two alcoholic beverages a day, limit your total daily intake of acetaminophen to two grams.)

Exercise for thirty to sixty minutes a day. Any form of exercise that makes your heart pump faster—even walking—is helpful, because it increases blood flow to your whole body. Of course, always choose forms of exercise that your wounded body can handle—and that won't worsen your wound. For example, if your wound is on a joint, don't move that joint.

Drink lots of water. Not drinking enough water can starve your wound. When you're even slightly dehydrated, the blood flow to your fatty tissues is reduced, making it much harder for those tissues to heal.

Water is the very best thing you can drink. Yet most of us drink far less water than we need. The irony is that, with very few exceptions, water can't hurt you, no matter how much you drink. If you drink more than your body needs, you'll just pee it out.

For optimum healing and health, drink water often and pee often. If someone ribs you for peeing so much, tell them you're following a physician's advice.

Surprisingly, many other beverages will actually *dehydrate* you. All alcoholic beverages will. So will a double espresso, an energy drink with lots of caffeine, or any other highly caffeinated beverage.

Whatever else you drink, it's wise to mostly drink water—especially when you're healing.

Avoid caffeine. Caffeine causes your blood vessels to constrict, reducing blood flow. While you're healing from a wound, drink no more than one or two caffeinated beverages a day.

Eat well—including plenty of protein. Protein supports your immune system and helps repair your body's organs and tissues. Meat, poultry, fish, shellfish, cheese, milk, eggs, soy products, nuts, and legumes (beans, lentils, split peas, etc.) are all rich in protein.

It's especially important to eat a healthy diet as you heal. Healing of all types requires large amounts of metabolic energy. Good nutrition supports this energy.

Avoid large amounts of refined sugar—especially soft drinks. Putting lots of sugar into your body in a very short time gives you a short initial burst of energy, but then causes your blood sugar to drop dramatically, temporarily starving your cells—and slowing their ability to heal.

Don't use tobacco while you're healing. Nicotine in any form —including snuff, chewing tobacco, nicotine gum, and nicotine patches—closes up your capillaries, reducing blood flow and slowing the healing process.

Smoking presents an additional health problem: it creates carbon monoxide, which limits your hemoglobin's ability to carry oxygen. Worse, smoking is itself a form of wounding. It irritates the cells that line the tiny chambers in your lungs called *alveoli*, reducing their ability to exchange carbon dioxide for oxygen. Smoking can also increase the risk of infection.

When you're not wounded, a little nicotine now and then isn't so bad. If you're otherwise healthy, smoking a cigar or pipe once a month won't hurt you. In fact, I'll have an occasional cigar with friends myself. But when you're healing from a wound, it's best to stay nicotine free.

Get treated with acupuncture. Acupuncture is not a replacement for proper medical care. However, because it improves the body's energy and blood flows, it supports and promotes healing.

This makes it a worthwhile addition to many wound-healing regimens. I've received acupuncture myself and have found it quite helpful.

Much remains unknown about how and why acupuncture works. Some day soon we may have laboratory instruments that can accurately measure a variety of energy flows in the human body that we can't today. What currently seems puzzling or mystical may then become measurable and predictable. By the time I retire, I hope to see a machine that can scan your body and tell you exactly where your energy flows are blocked.

Get down from high altitudes. If you normally live at a low altitude but get wounded at a high one—say, above 5,000 feet—get back to your normal altitude as soon as you reasonably can. At higher altitudes, there's less oxygen in the air, which means that less oxygen gets into your blood; as a result, your wound will heal more slowly. (If you've been at that higher altitude for four to six weeks, however, by then your body will have automatically adapted.)

Wounds of All Types

Your body, mind, and spirit can all help each other to heal. Here are some simple, proven, time-tested techniques that will support your healing in multiple, mutually reinforcing ways.

Avoid re-wounding yourself. Look carefully and honestly at how you got wounded. Then do whatever is necessary to avoid getting wounded again in that same way, or by the same person or situation.

This may mean acquiring some form of protection—a bicycle

helmet, or a guard dog, or a can of mace. It may mean setting stronger boundaries—such as telling someone "Stop that!" or "Next time you do that, I'm leaving" or "If you try that again, I'm calling the police." It may mean getting out of a dangerous situation, and avoiding similar ones in the future. It may mean redefining or ending a relationship. It may also mean staying alert for clues that danger is afoot—when you walk home alone late at night, for example, or when your mother has her third drink at a family gathering.

Get extra sleep. Sufficient sleep is important to good health—and when you're wounded, your body needs extra sleep to handle the burden of healing. If you normally need eight hours, get nine. The ideal is to sleep whenever (and for however long) your body wants to.

Take plenty of vitamin A, vitamin C, vitamin D3, vitamin E, zinc, and omega-3 fatty acids. All of us need these on a regular basis—but when we're wounded we need more of them to heal properly.

Vitamin A reverses the negative effects of stress hormones on your immune system's wound healing response. For people with wounds, I recommend a *temporary* mega-dose of 50,000 international units (IUs) a day. (If you take this much vitamin A for six months, however, you could wound your liver.) When you're not wounded, I recommend 10,000 IUs daily.

Vitamin C and zinc are critical for building new tissue. If you're wounded, take 500 milligrams (mg) of vitamin C twice a day, and 220 mg of zinc sulfate twice a day as well.

Omega-3 fatty acids—the scientific name for the natural fat in fish and shellfish—provide important support for your immune system. If you've got a wound, take fish oil in either liquid or capsule form; take the amount recommended on the bottle. Or simply eat fish or shellfish once a day.

Vitamin D functions as a natural antidepressant, and several studies show that it is essential to proper brain function and psychological health. This makes it especially important for psychological and spiritual healing. There's also some preliminary evidence that vitamin D can blunt the symptoms of seasonal affective disorder (SAD). Getting enough vitamin D is especially important for people living north of the fortieth parallel, where winter days are quite short.

Most of us get plenty of vitamin D in our food—but sunlight is required to transform the vitamin D we eat into a form that's biologically active. D3 is the synthetic form of this. I recommend taking 1,000 IUs of vitamin D3 a day under normal circumstances, 2,000 IUs if you have a wound. If you live in a locale where the winter days are quite short, take 2,000 IUs daily throughout the winter, even if you're not wounded.

One last note on vitamins: to heal properly, we need to do more than pop pills. Please don't take vitamins while ignoring the other suggestions in this chapter.

Spend a few minutes a day breathing deeply. Deep breathing increases both blood flow and the flow of spiritual and psychological energy. I can't overstress how helpful—and how simple—this practice is. After a decade of practicing deep breathing, I'm still amazed at how quickly I can relax and clear my head just by taking a few slow, present, deep breaths.

I normally do this for three to five minutes a day—ten when I'm wounded. I also stop and breathe deeply for a few minutes whenever I'm feeling stressed or tense. But even thirty seconds of deep breathing can make a noticeable difference.

The process takes only a few breaths to master. Close your eyes, breathe in deeply, and follow your breath as it flows in through your nose, down your throat, deep into your lungs, and then back out again.

Some people like to follow the energy of each inhalation all the way down into their bellies. That's fine, too. The air doesn't flow beyond their lungs, of course—but the spiritual and psychological energies continue flowing into their centers of gravity, behind their navels.

Each day, spend thirty minutes or more meditating or quietly relaxing. This relaxes your capillaries, increases your blood flow, and promotes the flow of psychological and spiritual energy. It also gives your body, mind, and spirit some deep rest. There are many different forms of meditation, but nearly all produce these benefits.

One simple way to meditate is to sit with your back straight (on the front of a chair, for example). Follow your breath as you did in the deep-breathing exercise above, but breathe normally instead of deeply. When your attention wanders, as it often will, simply bring it back to your breath.

Each day, spend thirty minutes or more in a peaceful natural setting. Many studies show that natural settings promote healing and relaxation—though we don't yet know why. Whether you're in the middle of the forest or a city park, the benefits are the same.

Listen to your body and follow its guidance. Your body will tell you what it needs to heal. If it asks for extra sleep, sleep longer. If it asks for a massage or gentle movement, do that. If it wants to weep, let yourself weep. (Weeping can help clean out psychological and spiritual wounds.) If it wants more protein or carbs or raw vegetables, eat those; if it doesn't want food at all for a short period, don't eat (but do drink plenty of water).

Give yourself permission to heal. Some folks are afraid to stop, rest, and heal for more than a day or two. Others are so used to keeping busy that doing nothing feels frightening or sinful. Still others feel guilty when they're not doing something productive.

But healing is not a sin, a form of laziness, or a sign of weakness. *When you're wounded, rest and healing are what your body, mind, and spirit need.*

I recently had dinner with a high-powered lawyer who had had major lung surgery two weeks earlier. After about ninety minutes, he said he needed to leave and get some rest. Then he apologized for not being able to stay. I congratulated him on listening to his body and making healing a priority. I said, "You recently had major surgery. You need six to eight weeks to rest and heal. That's how long it takes before you can go back to work. If you don't take the time off and let your body rest, it's going to be a year before you're back to normal. Take the time off and let your body do what it needs to do. That's what will get you back to normal the fastest."

Accept the necessary pain of healing. To heal physically, psychologically, or spiritually, we must be willing to acknowledge and experience some pain.

It's okay to take painkillers to blunt serious physical pain. But don't take more pain-reducing drugs than you genuinely need. As for psychological and spiritual pain—grief, fear, disappointment, loneliness, etc.—the more you let yourself accept it and feel it, the faster you will heal. If you try to avoid the pain through mood-altering drugs, alcohol, sex, compulsive behavior, or denial, you will drag out the healing process—and, paradoxically, increase your pain.

Stay connected to people who care about you. One of your biggest sources of healing is someone who cares about you, provides support, and, if necessary, takes care of you. If you have one or more such people in your life, allow them to help you. Ask for their help if they don't automatically offer it—and be as specific as you can. *Would you massage the area around my wound for me each morning for fifteen minutes? Can you drive me to my medical appointment? Would you pick up a prescription for me? Could you help me change my dressing?* Also ask for—and accept—the help of your Higher Power.

Love and accept yourself. Whatever your past experience, you can start doing this right now.

If a wound hasn't healed within two weeks, consult a professional. Any wound so large, deep, or chronic that it lasts more than fourteen days is cause for concern. See a healing professional promptly.

CHAPTER 12

Getting the Right Help

As we've seen, most small wounds heal on their own without professional help. But many larger wounds—whether they're physical, psychological, or spiritual—need care and treatment from a talented healing professional.

If you become wounded and need immediate treatment, go straight to the nearest emergency room or urgent care center. But if there's less urgency, take your wound to a healing professional you've worked with before—someone you know and trust. Because they are familiar with your health history and personality, they are in an ideal position to help you heal. (And if, for some reason, they can't help you with your wound, they can often refer you to the right person.)

It's best if you can see the same healing professional at all stages of your healing. Because this person will have an ongoing relationship with your wound, they can tell immediately if it is healing properly, or if there is a problem.

If your clinic or HMO discourages you from seeing the same professional, and tries to schedule you with whomever is available, push back: "I'd like to see Dr. _____ again next time, please. They're familiar with the wound, so they're the best judge of how well it's healing. When is their next available appointment?"

If you don't know of a healer you can trust with your wound, ask for recommendations from people you *do* trust—doctors, psychotherapists, spiritual leaders, family members, other healers, friends, neighbors, colleagues, etc. Describe your wound and ask, "If you had this wound yourself, who would *you* see—and why would you choose them?"

If you have a serious physical wound that requires the help of a surgeon, take this additional step: call the operating room of a nearby hospital, speak with an OR nurse, say what kind of surgery you will need, and ask them to recommend one or more surgeons. The OR nurse will know from long experience which surgeons do the best work.

Helping Healers Help You

How you interact with any healing professional can have a profound effect on how you heal. Here are some helpful guidelines:

If you can, take a picture of your wound soon after you get it, and every day or two thereafter. Show these photos to your healer at each appointment. Or, if you prefer, measure your wound daily and write down how it changes day by day.

If you have a serious physical wound, bring a family member, friend, or neighbor with you to appointments. This person can raise issues and ask questions that might not occur to you. Later on, they may also remember information that you forgot.

Some people keep track of details in a different way, by using their smartphones or iPads to record their conversations with healers. If you decide to do this, *always* ask the healer's permission first. Be aware that some healing professionals will say no, not because they're second rate, but because they're worried about being sued—an understandable concern in this litigious world.

Cut the healer some slack if they arrive late for your appointment. Every good healer tries to stay on time—but they never know what the next hour or patient will bring. Appointments can run long; they may receive an urgent phone call; a patient may faint during an exam. By late afternoon, healers often run at least an hour late.

This principle is doubly true for those of us who do surgery. One morning I was called in to do emergency surgery before dawn. I was an hour late for my 7:30 appointment, and when I walked in, the patient asked me, "How can you be an hour late for your first appointment of the day?" I told her, "I'm sorry to make you wait—but I just saved somebody's life. If, next time, you're the one on the operating table, I promise you that I'll take as much time as I need to save your life."

In general, the earlier in the day you can schedule an appointment, the more likely your healer is to be on time.

Don't ask healers for personal information about themselves. It's okay to spend a minute or two chatting before getting down to business. But don't ask healers about their marital status or kids or personal lives. Many keep such information private. You can, however, ask questions related to their work, such as "How long have you been practicing?" or "Where did you do your medical training?" or "When did you open this office?" or "What do you most love about your work?"

Good healers will ask *you* for personal information, however—about your health history, your family, your lifestyle, your work, what you do for fun, etc. This information helps them to better understand your wound and to create the right treatment plan for it. (If a question seems too personal, it's okay to say, "Why do you want to know that?" or to simply decline to answer.)

Tell the healer the story of how you got wounded. The more a healing professional knows about how you got your wound, the more they can help you. So don't just show them your wound and ask for help. Briefly explain the entire sequence of events: what led up to the wound; where you were at the time; what you were thinking and feeling; what you did; what other people did; how long it has been since you got the wound; and what has happened during that time. Be as clear and straightforward as you can; don't exaggerate, make up details, or leave out anything important. End your story with how you feel right now.

If a healer doesn't ask for the story behind your wound, *tell it to them anyway.* If they refuse to hear it—or insist that they don't need to—find a different healer.

Why is the story behind a wound so important? Consider Amina and Raul, who have shoulder wounds that look almost identical. But Amina got her wound this morning, while Raul's is four months old and won't heal. Amina was wounded when she fell off her roof, while Raul's wound is the result of nerve damage.

Amina's and Raul's wounds require very different treatment plans. Yet in order for a healer to design the right plan for either person, they need to hear that person's story.

One last point about telling your story: in the United States, under federal law, a healing professional must keep confidential everything you tell them. They can't share the information with anyone, even a trusted colleague, without your explicit permission. The only exception is if they believe you present a danger to yourself or someone else—in which case they *must* report the information to the relevant authority.

If a healer doesn't pay close attention to you, ask them to. Part of being a good healer is being fully present with each patient or client. If your healer reads their notes or looks at a computer screen while you tell your story—or, worse, tries to complete your story for you—say to them, "I need you to listen to me." If they still don't give you their full attention, leave and see someone else.

Also make sure that the healer looks closely at your wound, not just at lab results or computer readouts. Numbers and scans give healing professionals important information, but they are no substitute for a careful visual exam.

Pay close attention to the healer. Use your ears, eyes, heart, *and* gut. Being fully present will help you become as knowledgeable as possible about your wound, your treatment options, and the healing process. It will also help you pick up clues about the healer. If, during your appointment, your gut says, *Something's wrong here*, listen to it. Challenge the healer; ask them questions; or even get up and leave if your gut prompts you to.

If necessary, give your healer guidance. If they haven't heard an important piece of your story, say so: "I'm not sure you heard me fully. Here's what happened next...." If they're looking in the wrong spot, tell them: "The pain isn't there; it's about two inches higher." Most important of all, when something that they do feels painful, tell them.

Agree on your therapeutic goals. It's essential that you and your healer understand and agree on the desired outcome of your treatment. Be clear and specific about what you hope for and expect. The healer then needs to tell you if they think your hopes or expectations are reasonable—and, if the healer believes they're not, to explain why they're not, and to suggest alternative goals. Together, the two of you need to get clear on whether you expect the wound to heal fully; how much functionality you expect the area to regain; how you expect the area to look or feel once it has healed; how long the process will take; and so on. If you and a healer can't agree on therapeutic goals, you need to either change your expectations or see a different healer.

Ask questions. If you need more information, ask for it. If you don't understand something, ask the healer to explain it. If they explain it and you still don't understand, ask them to explain it again in a different way.

Also ask questions to gather information. By the end of your second appointment, get answers to these questions:

- *Can this wound be healed?* No healer can give you a definitive answer—but they *can* say, "There's a very good chance" or "Most wounds like this do heal" or "I don't know, but it's certainly possible, and I'm very willing to try."

- *Have you seen a wound like this before?* The vast majority of the time, the healer will say yes. But if they say no, their answer to the next question is especially important.

- *Are you the best person to help me heal this wound, or should I see someone else?* If the healer is not trained in the healing technique you need—or if they know of someone else who can do a better job—it's their responsibility to refer you to a different professional who can best help you heal.

- *What do I need to do?* Get clear, detailed instructions on how to care for your wound, what medications and/or supplements to take, etc. If the healer offers you two or more alternatives to choose from, also ask, *If someone close to you had this wound, which alternative would you recommend to them?*

- *What should I not do?* Sometimes knowing what to avoid— or what to stop doing—can be critical to healing a wound.

- *What can my family and friends do to help?* Healing is often a team effort. Here are some things others can do:

- Remind you when it's time to change a dressing or take your medication.
- Remind you of upcoming appointments.
- Get you to and from those appointments.
- Join you at those appointments.
- Change the dressing on your wound.
- Massage the area near your wound.
- Take pictures of your wound as it heals.
- Run errands for you.
- Cook for you.
- Nag you to follow your treatment plan.
- Provide a loving, healing presence.
- Lovingly confront you when you don't follow part of your treatment plan.
- Leave you alone (when doing so supports your healing).

  If you don't have family or friends who can help, ask your neighbors; or speak with a leader at your church or synagogue or mosque; or contact a local social service agency such as Catholic Charities, Lutheran Social Services, or Jewish Family Services. (These agencies serve people of all faiths.)

- *How long do wounds like this normally take to heal?* Expect a clear, limited range—e.g., four to five weeks—for physical wounds. Expect a much wider range—e.g., usually months, and sometimes years—for psychological and spiritual wounds.

- *If my wound heals normally, what can I expect to happen in the days and weeks to come?* The healer should give you a brief time line that includes descriptions of multiple stages of healing.

If a healer acts arrogant or dismissive, see someone else. A good healer is both confident and humble: confident about their own abilities and knowledge, but also humble, because they know that they are not in control of your healing.

None of us knows for certain what will heal and what won't. We healers can do our best for you, but without your cooperation *and* the support of a Higher Power, you won't heal.

Unfortunately, some healers—especially physicians—become arrogant. I've watched my colleagues diagnose people without even looking at their wounds. I've also seen them ignore people's questions, say curtly, "You're going to be fine; just do what I told you," and leave the room. Sadly, these healers are also the ones most likely to make serious errors.

If you don't get what you need or expect from a healer, say so. If, after being asked, the healer *still* doesn't provide what you need—or doesn't clearly explain why it's best for you *not* to get it—find a different healer.

Expect to be given a treatment plan by the end of your first or second appointment. This will include what the healer will do; what you need to do; what others can or should do to help; and what you can expect to happen, day by day, as you heal. The plan may be a detailed written document, or it may be as simple as "Change the dressing daily, and wear a helmet when you skateboard from now on," or "Let's meet monthly for a few sessions and work on helping you build clearer boundaries with your brother." Whatever the plan, review it carefully with the healer to ensure that you understand it. Then follow it.

If you see a healing professional about the same wound three times, but it keeps getting worse, see someone else. Some wounds—including psychological and emotional ones—may get worse for a short time before improving. However, if a wound doesn't turn around after three visits, something needs to change.

First, ask yourself: *Am I doing anything that's getting in the way of my healing?* If so, *you* need to change.

If not, you may need a different treatment plan, a different healer, or both. If your healer insists, "There's no problem with the treatment; you're going to be fine; just be patient," get a second opinion.

If you've seen two or more medical professionals about a physical wound, and it still won't heal, consult a wound healing specialist at a nearby wound care center, large hospital, or academic medical center. An experienced wound healing specialist may be able to quickly diagnose and treat a problem that has stumped other doctors. The best places to find these specialists are wound care centers. Many of these centers are in large hospitals; others are freestanding organizations. Wound healing specialists also work at medical centers affiliated with medical schools; such centers can be found all over the world.

CHAPTER 13

Caring for Your Scars

Once we heal from any significant wound, we carry a reminder of that wound with us for the rest of our lives. We call this reminder a scar.

Scars play a unique and invaluable role in physical healing, fulfilling two complementary functions at once. They create a tight seal that binds formerly wounded tissues together. They also separate the inside (your body) from the outside (your environment), and protect the inside from dangerous outsiders, such as bacteria.

Once scar tissue forms, it never goes away. A wound may have healed, but, because of the scar tissue, the area is less flexible and resilient than it used to be. If that spot gets repeatedly rewounded—for example, if you work on an assembly line and do the same movement over and over—then, over time, scar tissue can build up.

Wounds on joints usually take a long time to heal because we naturally tend to bend a joint, even a wounded one. As we pull and stretch the wounded area, it gets re-wounded. As a result, it takes longer to heal—and we create a bigger and bigger scar.

Scars don't re-create function; they just hold tissue together. The more scar tissue you have in any spot, the less functional that area is.

In general, wounds shouldn't be touched. Your body knows this, which is why it sends a strong message of pain whenever pressure is put on a wound. Unlike wounds, however, scars *should* be touched. Whether a scar is physical, psychological, or spiritual, when it is left untouched it will become stiff and immobile. However, regular, gentle massage can make it more supple, more pliable, and less painful.

Scars are very sensitive, especially fresh ones. Physical scars are full of very tiny nerves that are easily set off. At first, touching a scar sets off these nerves. But with regular massage, the nerves settle down and become less sensitive, and the scar stops being painful. It's the same process by which your skin got used to regular shaving. The nerves in the scar toughen up.

I have a large knee scar from an injury I got playing college football. At one point, this scar was so painful and sensitive that I couldn't bear to have my pants directly touch it. If I hadn't done something about it, eventually I would have had difficulty walking. Fortunately, I went to a healing professional—in this case, a massage therapist.

In our first session, she looked at my knee scar and said, "I'd like to massage this scar. It will help reduce the pain." I told her, "I'm worried that if you touch that scar at all, I might punch you, because it's way too painful to be touched." She said, "Just let me touch it lightly, for a short time. We'll start out gentle and easy." I took a deep breath and said okay.

She put oil on it, and she touched it extremely gently—but it still hurt like hell. I only let her massage it very lightly for a few seconds.

But next time she massaged it, a week later, the pain wasn't quite as bad, and I let her touch it a bit longer.

As the weeks passed, the pain in the scar slowly subsided. Each time she was able to massage it for a little longer, with a little more pressure. After about three months, the scar no longer hurt when she touched it; in fact, massaging it actually felt good.

That was fourteen years ago. Today, after years of regular massage, the scar is fairly soft and not at all painful. Most of the time I forget it's even there.

I learned a lot from that massage therapist. As a result, I always encourage my patients to massage their scars, or have someone else massage them. I say, "Keep your hands off your wounds, but put them on your scars."

Psychological and Spiritual Scarring

Psychological and spiritual scars serve the same function as physical scars: they protect us from harm by dangerous outside forces.

Let's suppose that, many years ago, you were wounded by an abusive relative, a mentally ill partner, or a hypocritical spiritual leader. Over time, with careful attention, compassion, and, perhaps, the help of a healing professional, you have healed from the painful experience. But a scar will still remain. This scar helps keep you safe by telling you what situations and people to avoid; when to set a personal boundary; and when to turn and walk away.

When you're in a situation that reminds you of a dangerous or damaging event from your past, your psychological or spiritual scar will throb painfully. This warning may cause you to stop, step back, and take stock of what's happening. The scar is a source of wisdom, safety, and protection.

But a scar of any kind is also a form of localized dysfunction. Unless it's attended to, it will stay stiff and immobile.

Most of us know someone who had an unhappy marriage, got divorced, and now says, "I'll never get married again." Or perhaps you know someone who was betrayed by their spiritual leader, and who now insists, "Religion is one big scam." These people were deeply wounded, and over the years they may have been able to heal from those wounds. But they also grew thick, inflexible scars that have closed them off to certain possibilities in their lives. These folks can benefit greatly from having their psychological and spiritual scars gently and regularly massaged.

Consider Marianne, who was wounded by a spiritual leader. She realizes that the best way to massage her scar is to attend services at a few congregations recommended by her friends. This scares her at first, but she reminds herself that she's just visiting; she doesn't have to sign up for anything or talk with anyone. She also promises herself that if anything makes her scar hurt, she'll get up and leave.

Over time, with each visit to a healthy spiritual community, Marianne's spiritual scar gets gently massaged, making it more supple and less painful. It takes some months, but eventually she finds a group that feels safe, loving, and spiritually nourishing to her. Eventually her experiences with these caring folks help Marianne to have a healthy spiritual scar—one that is flexible and pain free, but that protects her from further spiritual wounding.

Now let's consider Antonio, who swears he will never remarry. Antonio can lightly massage his psychological scar by going out on some relaxed, informal, low-pressure dates, such as a short meeting at a coffee shop, or a walk through the park.

Antonio's first date, with a woman named Caitlin, doesn't go well. The more they talk, the more Caitlin reminds him of his ex-wife, and the more their conversation mirrors past conversations that turned into arguments. So, after forty minutes, with his psychological scar throbbing, Antonio says good-bye. His scar has protected him.

His next date, with a woman named Lorraine, goes very well: he and Lorraine talk comfortably for over an hour. By the time they have finished their third coffees, Antonio thinks, *I can see myself falling in love with this woman.* He starts to ask Lorraine to join him for a walk along the nearby beach. Then his psychological scar starts to throb, and he realizes that it has received all the massage it can handle for the day. So he stops himself, and he and Lorraine exchange phone numbers and e-mail addresses. A week or so later, when his scar can handle more massage, he calls her again.

In the weeks that follow, Antonio pays close attention to his psychological scar, so that it gets massaged properly and he does not get re-wounded. He is careful not to rush into emotional or sexual intimacy with Lorraine.

On their third date, he tells Lorraine about his marriage and divorce, and explains to her that he is in no hurry to begin a new romance. At first this bothers her, and she asks him, "Why? Are you afraid of women?" Antonio's scar immediately begins to throb. But as they talk more, Lorraine explains that she used to be involved with an emotionally distant man. She admits that Antonio's words made *her* psychological scar flare up. They talk further, slowly revealing more about their pasts, their scars, and their vulnerabilities. Eventually Antonio realizes that they have begun gently massaging *each other's* psychological scars.

After an hour of intense personal talk, Antonio says, "That's about all the massage my scar can handle right now. Let's get some supper and talk about something trivial—like our favorite bands." Lorraine smiles and agrees.

CHAPTER 14

Healing as a
Way of Life

In every moment of our lives, we all have the power to heal.

The vital power that can heal us is one of nature's strongest forces. It is built into every cell in our body, every neuron in our brain, and every aspect of our soul.

As science continues to advance—and as ancient healing tools become rediscovered—many of us will be able to heal from wounds that may be unhealable today. In 1985, no one imagined how the discovery of growth factors, the development of EMDR, or the proliferation of nonreligious spirituality would revolutionize human healing. More and bigger revolutions are on the horizon—and entirely unpredictable ones will surely follow.

None of these advances will make us immortal, of course. Eventually our bodies will wear out and die. But even death offers us an opportunity for spiritual healing.

Because we all can heal, we can all also have hope.

Our Unprecedented Gifts

Most of us who live in the twenty-first century have been given three huge gifts: knowledge, safety, and time.

Knowledge. We healers know so much more about healing and the human organism than we used to. We have tools and treatments that seemed unimaginable or out of reach only a decade ago. Much of what we do today to help ourselves heal—from acupuncture to growth factors to spiritual rehabilitation—would have looked like magic to an American of half a century ago.

Each new scientific discovery reveals how complex and exquisite our bodies, minds, and spirits are. Every time we unlock another of the universe's secrets and swing open a door, we discover a new set of even more astonishing secrets behind it. The more we learn, the more awed we become, and the more we realize we don't know.

This knowledge both humbles and heals us. We learn that we cannot control the world, or even our individual lives; we also learn that, in healing, human trust, caring, focus, and generosity are more important than control.

We are also continually humbled by some of the ancient healing tools and practices that we are only now rediscovering, after ignoring them for decades or centuries. A thousand years ago, for example, Vikings and Native Americans used sphagnum moss to prevent the spread of infection; now, in the twenty-first century, we are once again employing it to promote healing.

Safety. Life for most human beings today is far less dangerous than it was in the past. Some infectious diseases have been wiped out; others are well on their way to eradication. We can quickly move healing professionals, treatments, and supplies almost any-where in the world—though we do not always have the political will or the money to do everything we should. We have systems to warn us of potential earthquakes, tsunamis, volcanic erup-tions, hurricanes, tornadoes, and disease pandemics; we also have sophisticated recovery plans to follow when any of these occurs. Our cars, trains, and airplanes get safer almost every year. In the twenty-first century, humankind's greatest threats are all of our own creation: war, terrorism, genocide, and organized crime.

Time. For thousands of years, most human beings lived for only four or five decades; many died as infants or children. Throughout these millennia, all but a privileged few spent their lives work-ing, raising families, and trying to survive in the face of disease, predators, war, and harsh weather. People usually died soon after their children grew up, if not before. Few had the time or energy to heal from their psychological and spiritual wounds—or to even acknowledge their existence.

Today, this has changed dramatically for most of us. The great majority of us will live seven, eight, or nine decades, and a signifi-cant minority will live for more than a century. Most of us will retain our psychological and spiritual faculties until very close to our deaths. Unlike the billions of people who came before us, many of us will master a profession, raise a family, and still enjoy several more decades of life.

We can use these precious extra years to grow, to learn, and to heal our wounds, especially our persistent psychological and spiritual wounds. Most of us have far more of these than we do chronic physical wounds.

We can also use this time to heal our wounded relationships—and, in doing so, to help the other people in those relationships to heal their own wounds. We can take the time to reflect; to care for each other; to learn from our mistakes; to integrate what we learn into our bodies, minds, and spirits; and to become more human.

Each of us has a choice: to embrace this grand opportunity, or to flee from it and further wound ourselves and others.

By now it's probably clear that healing and growth never end. We never reach a place where we can say, "Aha! That's it! I'm fully healed. My life is complete." Often we'll face a set of challenges; we'll work through them over time; and, in the process, we'll heal from a painful (and perhaps chronic) wound. Then, after a brief respite—which, in my experience, lasts anywhere from ten minutes to three months—a new set of challenges will emerge, and we'll discover another old wound that needs to be healed.

Healing Through Relationship

Relationships are all about wounding and healing.

As we grow up, learning, wounding, and healing form a single ongoing process. Each day, as we interact with other people, we try out new behaviors and ideas. Some of these bring us rewards; others wound us. We learn from the experience, do our best to heal, and then take new risks with the people in our lives. Over time, we learn who is safe and trustworthy, who isn't, what behaviors and ideas work, and which ones don't.

As adults, we continue this process, but we also forge intimate relationships in order to heal. We give each other care and support and pleasure—and sometimes we wound each other. Through these interactions, we often discover old wounds in ourselves that we didn't know we had. Over time, if we're mindful, we can use these relationships to explore each wound, discover its boundaries, and clean it out. We can then experience deep, sustained healing.

In the relationships we choose, we thus have the opportunity to heal wounds we received in the past, especially in relationships we *couldn't* choose—i.e., with the members of the family that raised us.

In creating healthy relationships as adults, and in choosing healing over re-wounding, we can change the course of our lives. We can rewrite the story of an old wound into a story of healing and recovery. Thus we can be reborn—not in some other body or life or realm, but in the here and now, where someone who cares for us replaces someone from our past who wounded us.

We can make this choice over and over—with other people, with our Higher Power, and with ourselves.

You, Me, and Microbes

It's midnight. The aromas of apple blossoms and freshly mown grass float into our bedroom through the open window.

I lie on my side with my arms around my sleeping wife. Her back is against me, gently pressing against my chest and belly each time she inhales. In her sleep she sighs and shivers, then pulls my arm tighter around her.

Outside our home, I can sense the trees, the grass, and the shoots in our recently planted garden. Everything is growing in its own unique expression of the vital force that envelops us all.

I'm wide awake, filled with amazement and gratitude—to all the people who helped me heal, and to my Higher Power. After all the abuse of my childhood, a learning disability, depression, multiple addictions, two failed marriages, and the multitude of ways I re-wounded myself as an adult, here I am at age sixty-one—psychologically and spiritually healthy, professionally successful, willing and able to help other people heal, and holding the woman I love, and who loves me, in my arms. I feel special, as if I've been singled out as the poster guy for the power of healing. After all, if even I can heal, anyone can.

I close my eyes and sigh—then suddenly open them again when I realize I've made a big mistake.

I'm not special at all.

My story is miraculous—but it's also as common as microbes. I'm only one of innumerable examples of how the vital force behind all life transforms wounds into healing, and turns pain into growth.

Every living creature seeks to heal and grow. Every living thing gets wounded, over and over. Every living organism embodies the same vital, omnipresent force. Each of us is only a tiny part of this ever-changing web of life.

I feel at once greatly humbled, thoroughly amazed, and deeply loved.

Acknowledgments

Most of the important events in my life have been collaborations. This book is no exception.

Some years ago, Wheaton College, my alma mater, invited me to give a talk. That talk, "Lessons Learned from the Healing Wound," was the seed that grew into this book.

Dr. Thomas Hunt taught me about the biology and clinical science of wounds and healing when I worked with him at the University of California–San Francisco Medical Center. Dr. Richard Simmons suggested that I start a wound healing clinic soon after I began teaching and practicing medicine at the University of Minnesota. My thanks to both gentlemen.

I'm grateful to Vance Fiegel, my laboratory manager, business partner, and friend, who commented on and double-checked the science in this book.

Thanks to my therapists, Gina Lewis at Sierra Tucson and Mic Hunter. Beginning in 1986, you guided me through much of my own psychological healing. Both of you helped me more than you know with this book.

Scott Edelstein, my editor, agent, and friend, helped this book grow from a fetus into a healthy adult. In the process, he also discovered several literary stem cells that I expect will differentiate into other helpful books and articles. Michele Matrisciani, my editor at Health Communications, "totally got" (her words) this book and helped make it a reality. Thanks to you both.

Finally, my profound thanks to my family: my children, Andrew, Emma, and Nicholas, and, most important, my wife, Florence, whose help and support made this book possible. Florence also did a great deal of work on the e-book version of this volume.

Index